Your First Steps into Programming: A Beginner's Guide to Building Software

Dan C. Cruz

Table of Contents

Introduction

Welcome to the exciting world of programming! If you're holding this book, chances are you're feeling a spark of curiosity about coding. Maybe you've seen headlines about technology, heard friends talk about building apps, or perhaps you have a problem you'd love to solve with software. Whatever the reason, you've taken the first step on a journey that can be incredibly rewarding, challenging, and ultimately, empowering.

For many people, the world of programming feels like a mysterious black box. We use computers, phones, and websites every single day, but how do they actually *work*? What goes on behind the screen? The answer, at its heart, is **code**.

What is Programming?

At its most basic level, **programming is the process of writing instructions for a computer to follow.** Computers are incredibly powerful, but they aren't smart on their own. They need precise, step-by-step instructions to perform tasks. These instructions are written in special languages that computers can understand (or translate), and the act of writing them is programming (or coding).

Think about writing a recipe. You list ingredients (data) and provide a sequence of steps (instructions) for someone to follow to create a dish (the desired outcome). Programming is similar, but your "ingredients" are data like numbers, text, or images, your "steps" are lines of code, and the "cook" is the computer, executing your instructions to produce a result, whether that's a calculation, a visual on a screen, or interacting with a database.

It's not about being a math genius or a computer wizard. Programming is fundamentally about **problem-solving** and **clear communication** – breaking down a large problem into smaller, manageable steps and then expressing those steps in a language the computer understands.

Why Learn to Code?

The reasons people learn to code are as diverse as the people themselves!

- **Career Opportunities:** Technology is integrated into nearly every industry, and the demand for people who can write software is high. Learning to code can open doors to new jobs or enhance your skills in your current field.
- **Bringing Ideas to Life:** Have an idea for an app, a website, a game, or a tool? Coding gives you the power to build it yourself. It turns you from a consumer of technology into a creator.
- **Understanding the Digital World:** In our increasingly digital lives, understanding the basics of how software works provides valuable insight and digital literacy.
- **Problem-Solving Skills:** Programming trains your brain to think logically, break down complex problems, and develop systematic solutions. These are skills valuable in any area of life.

- **Automation:** Learn to write scripts to automate repetitive tasks on your computer, saving you time and effort.
- **Creativity:** Coding is a deeply creative process! You start with a blank page (or screen) and build something from scratch.

For me, learning to code started as a way to automate some tedious data tasks at a job. I was tired of doing the same copy-pasting and calculations manually. The satisfaction of writing a script that did hours of work in seconds was exhilarating! That practical benefit quickly blossomed into a fascination with building things and solving problems in completely new ways.

Who This Book Is For

This book is written specifically for **absolute beginners**.

- You don't need any prior programming experience.
- You don't need to be a computer expert.
- You don't need a fancy computer (any modern laptop or desktop will do).
- You just need curiosity, willingness to learn, and patience.

If you've ever thought coding was too hard, too technical, or just not for you, this book is designed to show you otherwise. We'll start with the absolute basics and build up step-by-step.

What You Will Learn

By the end of this book, you will have a solid understanding of the fundamental concepts that are common to almost *all* programming languages. We won't focus on becoming an expert in one specific language (though we will use examples in one or more languages to illustrate points), but on the core ideas that form the foundation of programming.

You will learn:

- What code is and how computers understand it.
- How to set up your first coding environment.
- How to write and run your very first program.
- How to store and work with information using **variables and data types**.
- How to perform operations on data using **operators**.
- How to make your programs make decisions using **conditional statements** (if/else).
- How to make your programs repeat actions using **loops** (for/while).
- How to organize your code into reusable blocks using **functions**.
- How to work with collections of data using basic **data structures** (like lists).
- How to get **input** from a user and show them **output**.

- How to approach **problem-solving** like a programmer.
- Basic techniques for finding and fixing **errors** (debugging).
- And, we'll even build a small piece of software together!

These concepts are the universal grammar of programming. Once you understand them, picking up your second, third, or tenth programming language or diving into specific fields like web development or data science will be much, much easier.

How to Use This Book

This book is designed as a hands-on guide. Programming isn't just theoretical; it's a practical skill.

- **Read and Understand:** Take your time to read the explanations. We'll use analogies and clear language to make concepts accessible.
- **Type the Code:** Do not just read the code examples! Type them out yourself. This helps reinforce the syntax and build muscle memory.
- **Experiment:** Once you've run an example, try changing the code. What happens if you change a number? A word? A condition? Making mistakes and figuring out why they happened is a powerful way to learn.
- **Complete the Exercises/Mini-Project:** This is where you apply what you've learned to solve problems yourself.
- **Don't Get Stuck:** It's completely normal to feel confused or run into errors. Everyone does! If you get stuck, re-read the section, try the code again carefully, and don't be afraid to take a break and come back to it with fresh eyes.

This is your journey. Go at your own pace. Celebrate the small victories (like when your code finally runs without errors!).

Getting Ready

Before we dive into the first chapter, make sure you have:

- **A computer:** Any Windows, macOS, or Linux computer will work.
- **Internet access:** You'll need this to download some necessary software (all free!).
- **A code editor:** We'll talk about choosing one in Chapter 2, but having one installed will be helpful. VS Code is a popular and free choice.

That's it! No advanced degrees or expensive software required.

Chapter 1
Entering the World of Code

Alright, take a deep breath. We're about to step across the threshold into the world of code. It might feel unfamiliar, maybe a little intimidating, but remember, every single experienced programmer started exactly where you are right now. This first chapter is about getting oriented, understanding the lay of the land before we start using the tools.

1.1 What is Computer Programming?

As we touched on in the introduction, at its core, computer programming is about giving instructions to a computer. But let's get a little more specific.

Think about giving instructions to another person. You might say, "Go to the kitchen, open the fridge, take out the milk, close the fridge, pour a glass, and put the milk back." You're giving a sequence of clear, ordered steps.

Computer programming is precisely that, but the recipient is a computer, and the instructions must be even *more* precise and unambiguous. Computers can't guess, they can't infer, and they can't handle vagueness.

1.1.1 Code as Instructions

The instructions we write are called **code**, and they are written in a specific **programming language**. A program (or script, or software) is simply a collection of these instructions, organized to perform a particular task or solve a specific problem.

Each line of code is typically an instruction for the computer to do something, such as:

- Store a piece of information (like a number or some text).
- Perform a calculation (add two numbers).
- Compare two pieces of information (is this number bigger than that one?).
- Repeat a task multiple times.
- Get input from the user (like text they type).
- Show output to the user (like displaying text on the screen).
- Access or save data (like reading from a file or a database).

The beauty of code is that once you write these instructions, the computer can execute them incredibly quickly and reliably, repeating complex tasks millions or billions of times exactly as instructed.

1.1.2 The Role of the Programmer

So, if code is the instructions, what is the programmer's role?

The programmer is the **problem-solver** and the **translator**.

1. **Understand the Problem:** The first step is always understanding *what* you want the computer to do. What is the desired outcome? What information do you have to start with?
2. **Design the Solution:** Figure out the sequence of steps needed to get from the starting information to the desired outcome. This often involves breaking a big problem down into smaller, more manageable sub-problems. This is the core of algorithmic thinking – defining a clear process.
3. **Write the Code:** Translate that sequence of steps into the specific syntax of a programming language. This is where you write the lines of code.
4. **Test and Debug:** Run the code to see if it works as expected. Almost inevitably, there will be errors or unexpected results. Debugging is the process of finding and fixing those issues.
5. **Refine and Improve:** Make the code better – more efficient, easier to read, capable of handling more situations.

Your role as a programmer isn't just typing syntax; it's about thinking logically, designing processes, and being meticulous in translating those processes into instructions the computer can follow.

1.2 How Computers Execute Code

How does the computer actually *read* and *follow* the instructions you write? Computers fundamentally understand very low-level instructions (often just sequences of numbers, like 0s and 1s – machine code). The programming languages we write in are much easier for humans to read and understand than machine code. So, there's a translation step involved.

1.2.1 Compilers vs. Interpreters (Simplified)

Different programming languages use different methods to translate your human-readable code into something the computer's processor can execute:

- **Compilers:** Some languages (like C++, Java, Go) use a **compiler**. A compiler is a separate program that reads your entire code file(s) *before* the program runs, translates it all into machine code (or an intermediate format), and saves that translated version as a new executable file (like a `.exe` file on Windows). When you run the program, you run this pre-translated executable file. This process is called **compiling**.
- **Interpreters:** Other languages (like Python, JavaScript, Ruby) use an **interpreter**. An interpreter is a program that reads your code file *line by line* while the program is running, translating and executing each instruction as it goes. There isn't a separate, pre-compiled executable file created beforehand. This process is called **interpreting**.

Commentary: For a new programmer, the difference between compilers and interpreters might seem academic, but it affects how you run your code and how you find errors. Compiled languages generally catch more errors *before* the program runs (during the compile step), while interpreted languages catch errors *while* the program is running, potentially only when it hits the specific line with the error. Interpreted languages are often considered easier to get started with because you can typically just write code and run it directly without an extra compile step.

For this book, the exact mechanism isn't critical to understanding the fundamental programming concepts, but it's good background to know when you see terms like "compiled language" or "interpreted language."

1.2.2 Basic Program Flow

Regardless of whether a language is compiled or interpreted, computers generally execute instructions in a program in a straightforward manner:

1. **Sequentially:** They start at the first instruction and execute each subsequent instruction one after the other, in the order they appear in the code.
2. **Unless Told Otherwise:** This sequential flow can be altered by **control flow** structures (which we'll cover in detail in Chapters 5 and 6). These allow the program to:
   - Make **decisions** (e.g., "If this condition is true, do this block of code; otherwise, do that block of code").
   - **Repeat** a block of code multiple times (loops).
   - Jump to and execute a different block of code elsewhere in the program (**functions**).

So, you write a script as a sequence of steps, and the computer follows them from top to bottom, making decisions or repeating tasks when your code tells it to.

1.3 Programming Languages: Your Tools

Just like there are many human languages, there are many programming languages (hundreds, if not thousands!). They differ in their syntax (how you write the instructions), their features, and what they are typically used for.

Some common programming languages include:

- **Python:** Known for its readability and versatility (web development, data science, scripting). Often recommended for beginners.
- **JavaScript:** Primarily for front-end web development (running in the browser) but also used for back-end (Node.js).
- **Java:** Used for enterprise applications, Android mobile apps.
- **C++:** Used for game development, operating systems, performance-critical applications.

- **C#:** Used for Windows applications, game development (Unity).
- **Swift:** Used for Apple (iOS, macOS) app development.
- **Go (Golang):** Used for building scalable network services.

And many, many more!

1.3.1 High-Level vs. Low-Level Languages

Programming languages are often categorized based on how close they are to human language versus machine code:

- **Low-Level Languages:** Closer to machine code (e.g., Assembly, C). They give you more direct control over the computer's hardware but are harder for humans to read and write.
- **High-Level Languages:** Closer to human language (e.g., Python, JavaScript, Java). They abstract away many details of the computer's hardware, making them easier and faster for humans to write code in. This book will focus on concepts applicable to high-level languages.

1.3.2 Choosing Your First Language (Briefly)

The concepts you'll learn in this book are fundamental and apply regardless of the specific language. However, to practice and see the code in action, you'll need to use *some* language.

For beginners, languages like **Python** or **JavaScript** are often recommended due to their relatively simple syntax, large communities, and extensive resources. Python is known for being very readable, almost like English, while JavaScript is essential if you're interested in web development.

This book will explain the core concepts using simple, language-agnostic terms, but we will provide code examples in a popular beginner-friendly language (we'll assume Python for the examples throughout this book, as listed in the table of contents, but the concepts are transferable). The syntax will differ if you choose another language, but the *ideas* behind variables, loops, and functions will be the same.

My advice here is not to get too hung up on choosing the "perfect" first language. Pick one that seems interesting or is recommended for beginners, focus on understanding the fundamental concepts, and know that you can always learn others later!

1.4 The Mindset of a Programmer

More than just learning syntax, learning to program is about developing a certain way of thinking.

1.4.1 Problem Solving

This is arguably the most important skill. Programming *is* problem-solving. Given a desired outcome, you must break it down into the smallest, logical steps.

If the problem is "write a program to check if a number is even or odd," you break it down:

1. Get the number.
2. Divide the number by 2.
3. Check the remainder.
4. If the remainder is 0, it's even.
5. If the remainder is not 0, it's odd.
6. Tell the user the result.

This process of breaking down problems into algorithms is central to programming.

1.4.2 Attention to Detail

Computers are literal. A single typo, a missing comma, a misplaced parenthesis – these small errors (syntax errors) can cause your entire program to fail.

Developing attention to detail is crucial. You'll need to be precise in how you write your code and how you think about the steps involved in your solution.

1.4.3 Handling Errors

Your code will almost certainly not work perfectly the first time you run it. Errors happen. Good programmers don't get discouraged by errors; they see them as clues.

Errors tell you that the computer didn't understand your instructions or something went wrong while executing them. Learning to read error messages, understand what they mean, and systematically figure out *why* your code isn't working is a fundamental part of the programming process, called **debugging**.

Embrace errors as learning opportunities. They are your guide to figuring out how computers interpret your instructions.

My early programming experiences involved a lot of frustration with tiny syntax errors that I couldn't spot. Learning to read the error messages carefully (even when they seemed cryptic at first) and checking my code line by line was a skill that took time but became incredibly valuable. Patience and persistence are key virtues here!

You've just taken your very first step into the world of code by understanding its fundamental nature. You know that programming is writing precise instructions, what the programmer's role is, how computers execute code (simplified), what programming languages are, and some of the key mindset shifts that happen when you learn to code.

This conceptual foundation is essential. In the next chapter, we'll get practical. We'll set up a basic environment on your computer and write and run your actual very first program. Get ready – it's time to code!

Chapter 2
Your First Development Environment and Code

Alright! You've thought about what programming is and the mindset involved. Now, let's translate that into action. To write and run code, you need a place to do it – your development environment – and the tools to execute your instructions. This chapter is about setting that up and creating your very first program.

2.1 Setting Up Your Workspace

Think about a carpenter needing a workbench and tools, or a writer needing a desk and a pen/computer. As a programmer, you also need a dedicated space and specific tools to write and execute your code. This is your **development workspace** or **environment**.

Luckily, for most beginner programming, your computer already has almost everything you need. We just need to get comfortable with a couple of key applications.

2.1.1 Choosing a Code Editor

While you *can* technically write code in a simple text editor like Notepad on Windows or TextEdit on Mac, it's like trying to build a house with just a hammer. Code editors are specifically designed for writing code.

They offer features that make coding much easier:

- **Syntax Highlighting:** Different parts of your code (like keywords, variable names, text) are colored differently, making it much easier to read and spot errors.
- **Indentation:** Code editors help you properly indent your code, which is crucial for readability and, in some languages like Python, essential for the code to run correctly.
- **Autocompletion:** They can suggest code as you type, saving you time and preventing typos.
- **Error Detection (Linting):** Many editors can flag potential syntax errors or style issues *while you are typing*, before you even try to run the code.

Choosing a good code editor is a game-changer for productivity and reducing frustration. There are many excellent, free options available:

- **VS Code (Visual Studio Code):** Extremely popular, powerful, and versatile. Great for beginners and professionals alike. Available for Windows, macOS, and Linux. (Highly recommended if you don't have a preference).
- **Sublime Text:** A very fast and lightweight option.
- **Atom:** (Note: Atom is no longer actively maintained, but you might still encounter it).

My advice? Pick one that seems easy to install and has good reviews (VS Code is a solid bet). Download and install it. You'll spend a lot of time here, so finding one you like is important, but don't agonize over the choice too much initially. You can always switch later!

2.1.2 Understanding the Command Line / Terminal (Basics)

This is the tool that might feel the most unfamiliar if you're used to only clicking icons and using graphical interfaces. The **Command Line Interface (CLI)**, also known as the **Terminal** (macOS/Linux) or **Command Prompt** / **PowerShell** (Windows), is a text-based way to interact with your computer.

Instead of clicking on a folder icon, you type a command to change directory. Instead of dragging a file to the trash, you type a command to delete it.

Why do programmers use it?

- **Running Programs:** Many programming languages are executed directly from the command line.
- **Automation:** You can write scripts to perform tasks via the command line.
- **Access to Tools:** Many developer tools are command-line based.
- **Efficiency:** For certain tasks, typing a command is much faster than navigating through menus.

You don't need to become a command-line expert today, but you need to know how to open it and navigate to the folder where you save your code files, as this is how we'll run our programs.

- **On Windows:** Search for "Command Prompt" or "PowerShell" in the Start menu.
- **On macOS:** Search for "Terminal" in Spotlight (Cmd + Space).
- **On Linux:** Look for "Terminal" or "Konsole" or "gnome-terminal" in your applications menu, or use the keyboard shortcut Ctrl + Alt + T.

Once it's open, you'll see a prompt, usually showing your username and the current directory you are in (e.g., C:\Users\YourName> on Windows, or YourName@YourComputer:~$ on macOS/Linux).

Here are two essential basic commands:

- **ls** (on macOS/Linux) or **dir** (on Windows): Lists the files and folders in the current directory.
- **cd [folder_name]**: Changes the current directory. cd Desktop would move you into the Desktop folder. cd .. would move you up one directory level.

My first encounters with the command line felt like being dropped into a text-based maze! It seemed so complex compared to clicking. But slowly, as I needed to run programs or navigate quickly, I saw its power. Just knowing these two commands, ls/dir and cd, will be enough to get you started with running code from the terminal.

2.2 Running Your Very First Program ("Hello, World!")

The tradition for learning a new programming language is to start with a program that simply outputs the text "Hello, World!". It's a simple task that verifies your environment is set up correctly.

Let's write this program in **Python**. Remember, the core concepts are universal, but the syntax is language-specific. Python is chosen here because of its readability.

2.2.1 Writing the Code

Open your chosen code editor. Create a new file.

Type the following single line of code exactly as you see it:

```
print("Hello, World!")
```

Step Explanation:

- print: This is a built-in **function** in Python. A function is a named block of code that performs a specific task (we'll learn more about functions in Chapter 7). The print function's task is to display whatever you give it.
- (...): The parentheses after print are where you put the information you want the function to use or act upon. This information is called an **argument**.
- "Hello, World!": This is the **argument** we are giving to the print function. The text enclosed in double quotes (") is called a **string** – a sequence of characters.

This single line is an instruction: "Computer, use the print function to display the text 'Hello, World!'"

2.2.2 Saving the File

Now, save this file.

1. Go to File -> Save As... in your code editor.
2. Choose a location on your computer. I recommend creating a new, easy-to-find folder, perhaps named my_first_code, on your Desktop or in your Documents folder.
3. Give the file a name. Let's call it hello.py. The .py extension is crucial – it tells the operating system (and you) that this is a Python file.

Save the file in your chosen folder
(e.g., C:\Users\YourName\Desktop\my_first_code\hello.py or /Users/YourName/Desktop/my_fir
st_code/hello.py).

2.2.3 Executing the Program

Now, let's run this code using the Python interpreter. This is where the command line comes in.

1. Open your Terminal or Command Prompt.
2. Navigate to the folder where you saved hello.py using the cd command.
   - If you saved it in my_first_code on your Desktop, you might type:
     - On Windows: cd Desktop\my_first_code
     - On macOS/Linux: cd Desktop/my_first_code
   - Use ls or dir to confirm hello.py is in the list of files.
3. Now, run the Python interpreter and tell it to execute your file:

   ```
   python hello.py
   ```

   Note: On some systems, you might need to use python3 hello.py if the python command
   points to an older version of Python.

Press Enter.

If everything worked correctly, you should see this output directly in your terminal:

```
Hello, World!
```

Congratulations! You've just written and executed your very first computer program!

That moment, seeing the text appear on the screen exactly as I instructed the computer, felt like
magic the first time. It's a tiny step, but it proves you can write instructions the computer understands
and get it to do something.

2.3 Understanding Syntax

You wrote print("Hello, World!"). This particular way of writing the instruction follows
Python's **syntax**.

Syntax is the set of rules that define the correct structure and combination of symbols in a
programming language. It's like the grammar of a human language. If you break the rules of syntax,
the computer won't understand your instructions, and you'll get a **syntax error** when you try to run
the code.

In our "Hello, World!" example, the syntax rules included:

- Using the specific keyword print.
- Placing parentheses () immediately after the function name.
- Enclosing the text string "Hello, World!" within quotes (" or ').
- Not putting anything extra at the end of the line (like a semicolon, which some other languages require).

If you had typed pint("Hello, World!") (typo), print"Hello, World!" (missing parentheses), or print(Hello, World!) (missing quotes around the string), you would have gotten a syntax error.

For example, trying to run a file with pint("Hello, World!") would give you an error like:

```
Traceback (most recent call last):
  File "hello.py", line 1, in <module>
    pint("Hello, World!")
NameError: name 'pint' is not defined
```

This tells you there's an error on line 1, and the name 'pint' isn't recognized. Reading and understanding these error messages is a key skill (we'll cover this more in Chapter 11!).

Every programming language has its own unique syntax. A program written with correct Python syntax won't run if you try to interpret it as JavaScript, and vice-versa. Part of learning any new language is getting familiar with its specific syntax rules for variables, functions, loops, etc.

But the *ideas* – what a function is, what a variable is, what a loop is – are the same across languages. This book focuses on those universal ideas.

You've done it! You've set up your basic workspace, learned how to navigate directories in the terminal, written your very first program, and successfully executed it. You also got your first taste of programming syntax.

This is the foundational process for running *any* code. In the next chapter, we'll move beyond just printing text and learn how programs can store and work with information using variables and data types. Get ready to expand your programming vocabulary!

Chapter 3

Storing Information: Variables and Data Types

Alright! Your "Hello, World!" program ran successfully. You're officially a programmer (of a very simple program, but still!). Now, let's make things more interesting. Programs aren't just about following a script; they're about working with information that can change.

Think about filling out a form online. You type your name, your age, your email address. The website needs to remember *your* specific name, *your* specific age, and *your* specific email. It needs to store that information temporarily while it processes your request, and maybe store it permanently in a database later.

In programming, we use **variables** to store information.

3.1 What is a Variable?

A **variable** is like a labeled container in your computer's memory. You give the container a name (the variable name), and you can put a value inside that container. You can also change the value in the container later.

Imagine you have a box, and you write "User Age" on it. Inside, you put the number 30. "User Age" is the variable name, and 30 is the value stored in the variable. Later, if the user has a birthday, you can open the box labeled "User Age" and replace 30 with 31.

Variables allow your program to:

- Remember information provided by the user.
- Store the results of calculations.
- Keep track of the state of the program (e.g., how many times a loop has run).
- Hold information retrieved from files or databases.

3.1.1 Declaring and Assigning Variables

In many programming languages, you need to **declare** a variable (create the container) before you can use it, and then **assign** a value to it (put something in the container).

The exact syntax varies between languages, but the concept is the same. In Python, declaring and assigning often happen in one step using the equals sign =.

Let's open our code editor and start a new file, maybe call it variables.py.

```
# variables.py
```

```
# Declaring and assigning variables in Python

user_name = "Alice" # Assigning the string "Alice" to the variable user_name
user_age = 30        # Assigning the number 30 to the variable user_age
price = 19.99        # Assigning the number 19.99 to the variable price
is_logged_in = True # Assigning the boolean value True to the variable
is_logged_in

print(user_name)
print(user_age)
print(price)
print(is_logged_in)
```

Save the file. Open your terminal, navigate to the directory where you saved it using cd, and run it:

```
python variables.py
```

You should see the values printed:

```
Alice
30
19.99
True
```

Step Explanation:

1. user_name = "Alice": We create a variable named user_name and immediately store the text "Alice" in it.
2. user_age = 30: We create user_age and store the whole number 30.
3. price = 19.99: We create price and store the decimal number 19.99.
4. is_logged_in = True: We create is_logged_in and store the boolean value True.
5. print(...): We then use the print function to display the *value* stored inside each variable.

You can also change the value of a variable after it's been assigned:

```
# variables.py - Add to the bottom of the file

print("\n--- Changing Variable Values ---")
```

```
score = 100
print("Initial score:", score)


score = score + 50 # Update the score by adding 50 to its current value
print("Score after adding 50:", score)


score = 200 # Assign a completely new value
print("Score after assigning 200:", score)


greeting = "Hello"
print("Initial greeting:", greeting)
greeting = "Hi" # Change the text
print("Greeting after changing:", greeting)
```

Save and run again. The output will show the values changing.

3.1.2 Variable Naming Rules and Conventions

Programming languages have rules for what you can and cannot name your variables:

- Names usually must start with a letter or an underscore (_).
- Names cannot start with a number.
- Names can only contain letters, numbers, and underscores.
- Names are typically case-sensitive (myVariable is different from myvariable).
- You cannot use reserved keywords that are part of the programming language's syntax (like if, for, while, print, class).

Beyond the strict rules, there are also **naming conventions** – widely accepted practices in the programming community for how to name variables to make your code more readable:

- **Use descriptive names:** Choose names that clearly indicate what the variable stores (e.g., user_age is better than ua, temperature_fahrenheit is better than temp).
- **Be consistent:** If you choose a style (like snake_case where words are lowercase separated by underscores, common in Python), stick to it. Other languages might prefer camelCase (e.g., userName).
- **Avoid single letters (unless common convention):** x and y are sometimes used for coordinates, i and j for loop counters, but generally use more descriptive names.

My personal struggle when I started was coming up with good, descriptive names. It felt slow compared to just using a or b. But I quickly learned that looking back at my own code (or someone else's) weeks later was infinitely easier if the variable names actually *meant* something. It's worth the extra second to type customer_order_count instead of c.

3.2 Understanding Data Types

In our variable examples, we stored different *kinds* of information: text ("Alice"), whole numbers (30), decimal numbers (19.99), and True/False values (True). These are different **data types**.

A **data type** tells the computer what kind of data a value is and how it should be stored and manipulated. Different data types have different properties and operations you can perform on them.

Think about real life: you treat a street address (text) differently than a person's age (number), or whether someone is a registered voter (yes/no). You can do math on age, but not easily on an address.

Common basic data types you'll encounter in almost any language include:

3.2.1 Numbers (Integers and Floating-Point)
- **Integers:** Whole numbers (positive, negative, or zero) without a decimal point (e.g., 10, -5, 0, 1000). Used for counting, quantities, etc.
- **Floating-Point Numbers (Floats):** Numbers with a decimal point (e.g., 3.14, -2.5, 0.0). Used for measurements, prices, scientific values.

```python
# variables.py - Add to the bottom of the file

print("\n--- Numbers ---")

number_of_students = 25 # Integer
temperature = -10 # Integer
year = 2023 # Integer

pi = 3.14159 # Float
price = 99.99 # Float
percentage = 0.85 # Float

print(type(number_of_students)) # In Python, type() shows the data type
print(type(pi))
```

Step Explanation: We create variables storing different types of numbers. type() is a Python function that returns the type of a value or variable.

3.2.2 Text (Strings)

- **Strings:** Sequences of characters, used for text. Strings are typically enclosed in quotes (single ", double "", or sometimes triple """ """ quotes depending on the language and need).

```python
# variables.py - Add to the bottom of the file


print("\n--- Strings ---")

greeting = "Hello, World!" # String using double quotes
name = 'Alice' # String using single quotes
message = "He said, \"Hello!\"" # Using escape character \ for quotes inside
string
long_message = """This is a
multi-line
string.""" # Using triple quotes for multi-line strings in Python


print(type(greeting))
```

Step Explanation: We create variables storing text using different types of quotes. Strings are fundamental for names, messages, labels, and any non-numeric text data.

3.2.3 True/False Values (Booleans)

- **Booleans:** Represent logical values, either True or False. Used for conditions, flags, and logic checks.

```python
# variables.py - Add to the bottom of the file


print("\n--- Booleans ---")

is_active = True # Boolean True
has_permission = False # Boolean False
is_ready = (10 > 5) # The result of a comparison is often a boolean

print(type(is_active))
print(is_ready) # Will print True
```

Step Explanation: We create variables storing the boolean values True and False. We also see that the result of a comparison (10 > 5) is a boolean value (True).

3.2.4 Other Common Types (Briefly)

Many languages have other built-in data types for storing collections of data, such as:

- **Lists** (or Arrays): Ordered collections of items (e.g., [1, 2, 3], ["apple", "banana"]).
- **Dictionaries** (or Objects, Maps): Unordered collections of key-value pairs (e.g., {"name": "Alice", "age": 30}).

We will cover these important data structures in detail in Chapter 8. For now, focus on numbers, strings, and booleans.

Understanding data types is important because:

- It determines what operations you can perform (e.g., you can add numbers, but adding strings might concatenate them).
- It affects how much memory the computer allocates to store the data.
- Attempting to perform an operation on the wrong data type is a common source of errors.

3.3 Printing Output: Showing Information to the User

We used the print() function in "Hello, World!" and throughout this chapter to see the values of our variables. Showing output to the user is a fundamental part of many programs, whether it's text in a terminal, a graphical interface, or a webpage.

3.3.1 Simple Print Statements

As you've seen, print() in Python displays the value given to it.

```python
print("This is a direct message.")
print(123) # Prints the number 123
print(True) # Prints the boolean True
```

3.3.2 Printing Variables

You can print the values stored in variables by passing the variable names to the print() function.

```python
my_value = "Some data"
print(my_value) # Prints the value of the variable my_value
```

You can also print multiple things by separating them with commas:

```python
name = "Bob"
age = 25
print("Name:", name, "Age:", age) # Prints: Name: Bob Age: 25
```

Commentary: In Python, using commas in print automatically adds a space between the items. Other languages have different ways to combine text and variable values for printing (often using plus signs + or special formatting).

The ability to print information is essential for seeing the results of your program's logic and is a primary tool for debugging (Chapter 11) – printing out variable values to understand what's happening inside your code.

You've made great progress! You now know how to use **variables** to store information in your programs, understand the rules for naming them, and recognize fundamental **data types** like numbers, strings, and booleans. You also know how to use the print() function to display the values of these variables.

These are foundational concepts – variables are the nouns of programming (the things we work with), and data types tell us what kinds of things they are. In the next chapter, we'll learn about **operators**, the verbs of programming, which allow us to *do* things with these values and variables, like performing calculations or making comparisons.

Chapter 4
Operators: Working with Values

Alright, you've got variables holding your data – names, ages, prices, whether someone is logged in. Now, how do we *use* that data? How do you calculate the total price of items in a shopping cart? How do you check if a user's age is greater than 18? How do you combine a first name and a last name?

This is where **operators** come into play. Operators are special symbols or keywords that perform operations on one or more values (or variables that hold values). The values that an operator works on are called **operands**.

Think of operators like the verbs in your program. Variables are the nouns (the things), and operators are the actions you perform *on* those things.

Let's open our code editor and create a new file, maybe call it operators.py, to try these out.

```
# operators.py


# We'll put examples for different operator types here
```

4.1 Arithmetic Operators

These are the operators you're probably most familiar with from math class. They perform mathematical calculations.

```
# operators.py - Add these examples


print("--- Arithmetic Operators ---")

# Let's start with some numbers
num1 = 10
num2 = 5
num3 = 3

# 4.1.1 Addition, Subtraction, Multiplication, Division
sum_result = num1 + num2
print("Addition:", sum_result) # Output: Addition: 15

difference = num1 - num2
print("Subtraction:", difference) # Output: Subtraction: 5
```

```python
product = num1 * num2
print("Multiplication:", product) # Output: Multiplication: 50

division_result = num1 / num2 # In Python 3, this is floating-point division
print("Division:", division_result) # Output: Division: 2.0

integer_division = num1 // num3 # Floor division (discards the fractional
part)
print("Integer Division (10 // 3):", integer_division) # Output: Integer
Division (10 // 3): 3

exponentiation = num1 ** 2 # 10 raised to the power of 2
print("Exponentiation (10 ** 2):", exponentiation) # Output: Exponentiation
(10 ** 2): 100

# 4.1.2 Remainder (Modulo)
# Gives you the remainder after division
remainder = num1 % num3 # 10 divided by 3 is 3 with a remainder of 1
print("Remainder (10 % 3):", remainder) # Output: Remainder (10 % 3): 1

# Modulo is useful for things like checking if a number is even (number % 2
== 0)
# or figuring out if a year is a leap year (more complex rules involve
modulo!)

# Arithmetic with floats
float1 = 10.5
float2 = 2.0
print("Float Addition:", float1 + float2) # Output: Float Addition: 12.5
print("Float Division:", float1 / float2) # Output: Float Division: 5.25
```

Save and run python operators.py. You'll see the results of each arithmetic operation printed.

Step Explanation: We used the standard symbols +, -, *, / for addition, subtraction, multiplication, and division. // performs integer division (rounding down to the nearest whole number). ** is for exponents. % is the modulo operator, giving the remainder of a division.

Commentary: These are straightforward, just like calculator buttons. Learning the modulo operator % is often new for beginners, but it's surprisingly useful in programming for tasks related to divisibility or cycling through sequences.

4.1.1 Order of Operations

Just like in mathematics, programming languages follow an order of operations (often remembered by acronyms like PEMDAS/BODMAS). Multiplication, division, and modulo are performed before addition and subtraction. Parentheses () can be used to override the standard order.

```python
# operators.py - Add these examples

print("\n--- Order of Operations ---")

result1 = 10 + 5 * 2     # Multiplication first: 10 + 10
result2 = (10 + 5) * 2   # Parentheses first: 15 * 2

print("10 + 5 * 2 =", result1) # Output: 10 + 5 * 2 = 20
print("(10 + 5) * 2 =", result2) # Output: (10 + 5) * 2 = 30
```

Save and run. The outputs clearly show how parentheses change the calculation order. Always use parentheses if you're unsure about the order or to make your intentions explicit, even if the default order would achieve the same result. It makes your code easier to read.

Arithmetic with other Data Types: Be aware that the + operator can also be used for string **concatenation** (joining strings together) in Python and many other languages.

```python
print("Hello" + " " + "World") # Output: Hello World
```

This is an example of operator **overloading** – the same operator symbol (+) doing different things depending on the type of data it's used with.

4.2 Assignment Operators

We've already used the most common assignment operator: the equals sign =. Assignment operators are used to store a value in a variable.

4.2.1 Assigning Values (=)

```python
# operators.py - Add these examples

print("\n--- Assignment Operator ---")
```

```python
my_variable = "some value" # Assigns the string "some value" to my_variable
another_variable = my_variable # Assigns the VALUE of my_variable to
another_variable

print(my_variable)
print(another_variable)
```

Step Explanation: The = operator takes the value on its right side and puts it into the variable named on its left side.

4.2.2 Compound Assignment (+=, -=, etc.)

These are shorthand operators that perform an arithmetic operation and an assignment in one step. They are a bit of convenience syntax.

```python
# operators.py - Add these examples

print("\n--- Compound Assignment Operators ---")

counter = 10
# counter = counter + 5 # Standard assignment
counter += 5 # Compound assignment: add 5 to counter, then store the result
back in counter
print("counter after += 5:", counter) # Output: counter after += 5: 15

amount = 50
amount -= 10 # Subtract 10 from amount, store result in amount
print("amount after -= 10:", amount) # Output: amount after -= 10: 40

price = 20
price *= 3 # Multiply price by 3, store result in price
print("price after *= 3:", price) # Output: price after *= 3: 60

# Works with strings too for concatenation!
message = "Hello"
message += ", World!" # Concatenate ", World!" to message, store result in
message
print("message after += ', World!':", message) # Output: message after += ',
World!': Hello, World!
```

Save and run. Compound assignment operators are very common and just a more compact way of writing variable = variable operator value.

4.3 Comparison Operators

Comparison operators are used to compare two values. They don't produce numbers or text; they produce a **boolean** value: either True or False. This is where the boolean data type we learned about becomes essential! Comparison operators are fundamental for making decisions in your code (Chapter 5).

```python
# operators.py - Add these examples


print("\n--- Comparison Operators ---")


x = 10
y = 12
z = 10
text1 = "hello"
text2 = "Hello" # Different capitalization!

# 4.3.1 Checking for Equality (==, !=)
print("x == y:", x == y)       # Is x equal to y? Output: False
print("x == z:", x == z)       # Is x equal to z? Output: True
print("x != y:", x != y)       # Is x not equal to y? Output: True
print("text1 == text2:", text1 == text2) # Is "hello" equal to "Hello"?
Output: False (case-sensitive)

# 4.3.2 Checking for Inequality (>, <, >=, <=)
print("x > y:", x > y)         # Is x greater than y? Output: False
print("x < y:", x < y)         # Is x less than y? Output: True
print("x >= z:", x >= z)       # Is x greater than or equal to z? Output: True
print("y <= z:", y <= z)       # Is y less than or equal to z? Output: False

# Comparisons with strings (based on alphabetical order)
print("text1 > text2:", text1 > text2) # 'hello' vs 'Hello'. Lowercase
letters have higher values than uppercase. Output: True
```

Save and run. The output will be True or False for each comparison.

Step Explanation: We use symbols like == (equal to), != (not equal to), > (greater than), < (less than), >= (greater than or equal to), <= (less than or equal to) to compare the values on either side. The result is always a boolean.

Commentary on == vs ===: You might encounter === (strict equality) and !== (strict not equal) in languages like JavaScript. In those languages, == checks only if the *value* is the same (potentially doing type conversion behind the scenes, which can be confusing, e.g., 5 == "5" might be true), while === checks if the *value* and the *data type* are *both* the same (e.g., 5 === "5" is false because one is a number, one is a string). Python's == operator is generally smarter and doesn't do surprising type coercions in the same way JavaScript's == does, so for most comparisons in Python, == is what you want to check if two values represent the same thing. Stick to == and != in Python for value comparison, but be aware of the concept of strict equality if you learn other languages later.

4.4 Logical Operators

Logical operators are used to combine boolean values or expressions that result in boolean values. They allow you to build more complex conditions.

```python
# operators.py - Add these examples

print("\n--- Logical Operators ---")

is_adult = True
has_ticket = False
is_vip = True


# 4.4.1 AND (and)
# Result is True only if BOTH sides are True
print("is_adult and has_ticket:", is_adult and has_ticket) # Output: False
print("is_adult and is_vip:", is_adult and is_vip)      # Output: True


# 4.4.2 OR (or)
# Result is True if AT LEAST ONE side is True
print("is_adult or has_ticket:", is_adult or has_ticket) # Output: True
print("has_ticket or is_vip:", has_ticket or is_vip)     # Output: True
print("has_ticket or False:", has_ticket or False)      # Output: False


# 4.4.3 NOT (not)
# Reverses the boolean value (True becomes False, False becomes True)
print("not is_adult:", not is_adult)       # Output: False
```

```python
print("not has_ticket:", not has_ticket) # Output: True

# Combining comparison and logical operators
age = 20
has_consent = True
can_enter = (age >= 18) and has_consent # (True) and (True)
print("Can enter (age >= 18 and has_consent):", can_enter) # Output: True

age = 16
has_consent = True
can_enter_again = (age >= 18) and has_consent # (False) and (True)
print("Can enter (age >= 18 and has_consent):", can_enter_again) # Output:
False

is_weekend = True
has_plans = False
can_relax = is_weekend and not has_plans # (True) and (True)
print("Can relax (is_weekend and not has_plans):", can_relax) # Output: True
```

Save and run.

Step Explanation: In Python, the logical operators are keywords: and, or, not.

- and: Checks if the condition on the left AND the condition on the right are both true.
- or: Checks if the condition on the left OR the condition on the right (or both) are true.
- not: Checks if the condition is NOT true (reverses the truth value).

Commentary: Logical operators are incredibly powerful for building complex decision-making logic. My "aha!" moment here was realizing I could combine multiple comparison checks
using and and or to create more nuanced conditions, like "Is the user over 18 *and* do they have a valid ticket?"

You've done great! You've learned about **operators**, the verbs of programming. You can perform **arithmetic** calculations, **assign** values to variables (including using shorthand compound operators), **compare** values using comparison operators (getting boolean results), and **combine** boolean results using **logical** operators.

These operators are fundamental tools for manipulating data and asking questions about values in your program. They are essential building blocks for the next big concept: **control flow**, which is all about making your program make decisions and repeat actions based on conditions, using the boolean results from comparisons and logical operations.

Chapter 5
Control Flow: Making Decisions

Alright, you know how to store numbers and text, do calculations, and compare values (which gives us those `True` or `False` boolean results). That's powerful! But imagine writing a program for a traffic light. It doesn't just follow the same sequence forever; it needs to decide: "If 60 seconds have passed *and* there are cars waiting, change to yellow. Otherwise, stay green." Programs need to be able to make choices based on different conditions.

This is the first major type of **control flow** we'll learn: **decision making**. Control flow is simply the order in which the computer executes the instructions in your program. By default, it's sequential (top to bottom), but control flow statements let you alter that.

5.1 The Need for Decision Making

Alright, we've built programs that can follow a sequence of steps. We can store data, do math, and print results. That's a good start! But imagine a program that's just a fixed script: always print "Hello", always add 5 to a number, always print the result. How useful is that in the real world? Not very, because the real world is full of conditions and variations.

This is why programs need the ability to **make decisions**. Decision making means executing different instructions or blocks of code based on whether a certain condition is true or false at a particular moment in the program's execution.

Think about everyday decisions:

- If it's raining, take an umbrella. Otherwise, don't.
- If you are hungry, eat something. Otherwise, wait.
- If your train is on time, proceed to the platform. Otherwise, check the delay information.

Each of these involves checking a condition ("is it raining?", "are you hungry?", "is the train on time?") and then choosing a path of action based on the outcome ("take an umbrella" or "don't").

Computer programs face these kinds of conditional situations all the time:

- **Responding to User Input:** If the user types "yes", do this. If they type "no", do that. If they type something else, ask them to try again.
- **Handling Different Data:** If the number is positive, perform this calculation. If it's negative, perform a different calculation. If it's zero, print a specific message.
- **Checking State:** If the user is logged in, show their profile. If they are not logged in, show a login form.

- **Validating Data:** If the email address format is valid, save it. Otherwise, show an error message.
- **Controlling Program Flow:** Continue a loop *if* a certain condition is still met. Stop a process *if* an error threshold is reached.

Without the ability to make decisions, a program would be completely rigid. It would run the exact same way every single time, regardless of the input it receives, the data it processes, or the state of the system it's running on.

My personal "aha!" moment with decision making was trying to write a simple text-based game. I quickly realized I couldn't just write a sequence of steps like "move north, pick up item, fight monster." I needed to check *if* the player could move north from their current location, *if* the item was actually there to be picked up, *if* the monster was still alive to be fought, and then do different things depending on those conditions. The game needed to adapt to the player's actions and the game world's state. Decision making was the key to that adaptability.

The core tools for enabling decision making in your code are **conditional statements**, most prominently the `if`, `elif`, and `else` statements we'll cover in the rest of this chapter. These statements allow you to specify a condition (something that evaluates to `True` or `False`) and then define blocks of code that the computer should execute *only if* that condition is met.

Understanding *why* this is necessary – because programs need to be flexible and respond to variations in data and circumstances – makes the syntax and structure of `if`/`else` statements much more meaningful. You're not just learning syntax; you're learning how to build intelligence and adaptability into your code.

That wraps up the conceptual need for decision making. You understand that programs require the ability to execute different paths based on conditions to handle variations in input, data, and state. This sets the stage for learning the specific syntax (`if`/`else`) to implement these decisions in your code, which is what we'll cover next.

5.2 Conditional Statements: If, Else If, and Else

The fundamental way to make decisions in programming is using **conditional statements**. The most common structure uses the keywords `if`, `else if` (or `elif` in Python), and `else`. These statements allow you to execute a block of code *only if* a certain condition is met.

Let's open our code editor and create a new file, `decisions.py`, to write some examples.

```
# decisions.py


# We'll write our decision-making code here
```

5.2.1 The `if` Statement

The simplest conditional statement is the `if` statement. It checks if a condition is `True`, and if it is, it executes the block of code immediately following it. If the condition is `False`, the block is skipped.

The condition inside an `if` statement is a **boolean expression** – something that evaluates to either `True` or `False` (like the comparisons we did in Chapter 4!).

In Python, the syntax looks like this:

```python
# decisions.py - Add these examples

print("--- The IF Statement ---")

temperature = 30

# Check if temperature is greater than 25
if temperature > 25:
    # This code block is executed only if the condition (temperature > 25) is
True
    print("It's a warm day!")
    print("Maybe wear shorts.")

print("This line runs regardless of the condition.")

print("\n--- IF Statement Example 2 ---")

age = 15

# Check if age is greater than or equal to 18
if age >= 18:
    # This code block is skipped because the condition (age >= 18) is False
    print("You are an adult.")
    print("You can vote.")

print("This line runs regardless of the condition.")
```

Save and run `python decisions.py`.

```
--- The IF Statement ---
It's a warm day!
Maybe wear shorts.
This line runs regardless of the condition.

--- IF Statement Example 2 ---
This line runs regardless of the condition.
```

Step Explanation:

1. We set `temperature` to 30. The condition `temperature > 25` evaluates to `True`. So, the code indented below the `if` statement is executed.
2. We set `age` to 15. The condition `age >= 18` evaluates to `False`. So, the code indented below that `if` statement is skipped entirely.
3. The lines outside the `if` blocks always run, regardless of whether the condition was true or false.

Important: In Python, the code block associated with an `if` (or `elif`, `else`, `for`, `while`, function definition, etc.) is defined by **indentation**. All lines at the same level of indentation below the `if` belong to that block. When the indentation goes back to the previous level, the block is finished. This is different from many other languages that use curly braces `{}` to define blocks. Correct indentation is *critical* for Python code to run!

5.2.2 The `else` Statement

What if you want to do one thing if the condition is `True` and a *different* thing if it's `False`? That's what the `else` statement is for. An `else` statement must come immediately after an `if` statement (or an `elif` statement).

```
# decisions.py - Add these examples

print("\n--- The IF-ELSE Statement ---")

number = 7

if number % 2 == 0: # Check if the remainder when divided by 2 is 0 (is it
even?)
    print("The number is even.")
else: # If the condition in the IF is False, this block is executed
    print("The number is odd.")
```

```
print("Finished checking.")


print("\n--- IF-ELSE Statement Example 2 ---")


is_sunny = False


if is_sunny:
  print("Let's go to the park!")
else:
  print("Let's stay inside.")
```

Save and run.

```
--- The IF-ELSE Statement ---
The number is odd.
Finished checking.


--- IF-ELSE Statement Example 2 ---
Let's stay inside.
```

Step Explanation:

1. `number % 2 == 0` evaluates to `7 % 2 == 0`, which is `1 == 0`, evaluating to `False`. The `if` block is skipped. The `else` block is then executed.
2. `is_sunny` is `False`. The `if` block is skipped. The `else` block is executed.

The `if` and `else` provide two mutually exclusive paths for the program to take based on a single condition.

5.2.3 The `else if` Statement (`elif`)

What if you have *more than two* possible outcomes based on multiple conditions? This is common. Maybe you want to check if a number is positive, negative, or zero. This is where `else if` (written as `elif` in Python) comes in.

An `elif` statement must come after an `if` statement and before an `else` statement. You can have multiple `elif` statements. The conditions are checked in order. The *first* condition that evaluates to `True` will have its corresponding code block executed, and then the rest of the `elif` and `else` chain is skipped.

```
# decisions.py - Add these examples
```

```python
print("\n--- The IF-ELIF-ELSE Statement ---")

grade = 85

if grade >= 90:
  print("You got an A!")
elif grade >= 80: # If the first condition (>= 90) was False, check if grade
is >= 80
  print("You got a B!")
elif grade >= 70: # If the previous conditions were False, check if grade is
>= 70
  print("You got a C.")
else: # If ALL the above conditions were False
  print("You need to study more.")

print("Finished grading.")


print("\n--- IF-ELIF-ELSE Statement Example 2 ---")

weather = "rainy"

if weather == "sunny":
  print("Great weather for a picnic!")
elif weather == "cloudy":
  print("Might need a light jacket.")
elif weather == "rainy": # This condition is True, so this block executes
  print("Bring an umbrella!")
else: # This else is never reached because "rainy" matched an elif
  print("Weather is unknown.")
```

Save and run.

```
--- The IF-ELIF-ELSE Statement ---
You got a B!
Finished grading.

--- IF-ELIF-ELSE Statement Example 2 ---
```

```
Bring an umbrella!
```

Step Explanation:

1. `grade` is 85. `grade >= 90` is `False`. `elif grade >= 80` (85 >= 80) is `True`. The block indented under this `elif` is executed ("You got a B!"). The remaining `elif` and the `else` are skipped.
2. `weather` is "rainy". `weather == "sunny"` is `False`. `elif weather == "cloudy"` is `False`. `elif weather == "rainy"` is `True`. That block executes ("Bring an umbrella!"). The final `else` is skipped.

The `if-elif-else` structure is your tool for handling multiple, mutually exclusive outcomes based on a sequence of conditions.

5.3 Working with Boolean Expressions

Remember from Chapter 4 that comparison operators (`>`, `<`, `==`, etc.) produce boolean values (`True` or `False`). Logical operators (`and`, `or`, `not`) also work with boolean values. The conditions inside `if` and `elif` statements can be any expression that *evaluates* to a boolean.

```python
# decisions.py - Add these examples

print("\n--- Working with Boolean Expressions ---")


temperature = 28
is_raining = True


# Condition using comparison and logical operators
if temperature > 25 and not is_raining: # (True and not True) -> (True and
False) -> False
    print("It's warm and not raining - perfect!")
else:
    print("Weather not ideal.")


# Example using variables directly if they are already booleans
is_paid = True
is_shipped = False


if is_paid and not is_shipped:
    print("Order is paid but not shipped.")
```

Save and run.

5.3.1 Combining Conditions

Alright, you know how if temperature > 25: works, or if user_age >= 18:. That's a single condition. But in the real world, decisions are rarely based on just one factor. You might decide to go to the park if it's **sunny** *and* it's a **weekend**. You might order pizza if you're **hungry** *or* it's **late**. You might *not* go outside if it's **raining**.

Programming allows us to combine those simpler True/False conditions (like temperature > 25 or user_age >= 18) using **logical operators**. These operators work specifically with boolean values (True and False) and let you build more sophisticated rules for your if and elif statements.

In Python, the most common logical operators are keywords: **and**, **or**, and **not**.

Let's open up our decisions.py file again and add some examples of combining conditions.

```python
# decisions.py - Add these examples


print("\n--- Combining Conditions with Logical Operators ---")


# Assume these variables hold boolean values or expressions that result in
booleans
is_sunny = True
is_weekend = False
is_hungry = True
is_late = False
is_raining = False


# Let's check combinations using the logical operators
```

The and Operator

The and operator checks if *both* the condition on its left side *and* the condition on its right side are True. If both are True, the result of the and operation is True. Otherwise, the result is False.

Think of it like needing *all* ingredients for a recipe. You need flour **and** eggs **and** sugar to bake a cake. If you're missing any one, you can't bake the cake.

```python
# decisions.py - Add to the section above


print("--- The AND operator ---")
```

```
# Condition: is_sunny AND is_weekend
# is_sunny is True, is_weekend is False. Both are NOT True.
can_go_to_park = is_sunny and is_weekend
print(f"Can go to park (sunny AND weekend)? {can_go_to_park}") # Output:
False

# Condition: is_hungry AND not is_late (We'll cover 'not' below, but imagine
it reverses is_late)
# is_hungry is True. Imagine not is_late is True (because is_late is False).
Both ARE True.
can_order_food_now = is_hungry and not is_late # (True and True)
# Let's actually use 'not' first for clarity below, then come back to this
combination!
```

Let's hold off on the second and example for a second and look at or and not first, then we'll combine them more effectively.

The or Operator

The or operator checks if *at least one* of the conditions on its sides is True. If the left side is True, or the right side is True, or *both* are True, the result of the or operation is True. The only way the result is False is if *both* sides are False.

Think of it like having options. You can get into the club if you have a ticket **or** you are on the guest list. You only need one of those things to be true to get in.

```
# decisions.py - Add to the section above

print("--- The OR operator ---")

# Condition: is_hungry OR is_late
# is_hungry is True, is_late is False. At least one is True.
can_order_pizza = is_hungry or is_late
print(f"Can order pizza (hungry OR late)? {can_order_pizza}") # Output: True

# Condition: is_raining OR is_late
# is_raining is False, is_late is False. Neither is True.
need_umbrella_or_hurry = is_raining or is_late
print(f"Need umbrella OR hurry? {need_umbrella_or_hurry}") # Output: False
```

The not Operator

The not operator is a unary operator, meaning it only works on a single condition. It simply reverses the boolean value of that condition. If the condition is True, not makes it False. If the condition is False, not makes it True.

Think of it like saying "Is it *not* raining?". If is_raining is True, not is_raining is False. If is_raining is False, not is_raining is True.

```python
# decisions.py - Add to the section above

print("--- The NOT operator ---")

# Condition: not is_sunny
# is_sunny is True. not reverses it.
is_not_sunny = not is_sunny
print(f"Is it NOT sunny? {is_not_sunny}") # Output: False

# Condition: not is_raining
# is_raining is False. not reverses it.
is_not_raining = not is_raining
print(f"Is it NOT raining? {is_not_raining}") # Output: True
```

Using Combined Conditions in if/elif

Now that we understand and, or, and not, we can use them directly in the condition part of our if and elif statements. The code block will execute only if the *entire combined condition* evaluates to True.

```python
# decisions.py - Add these examples

print("\n--- Combined Conditions in IF Statements ---")

temperature = 28
is_raining_now = False # Changed variable name slightly for clarity
day_of_week = "Saturday"

# Condition: temperature > 25 AND it's NOT raining AND it's the weekend
# (28 > 25 is True) AND (not False is True) AND ("Saturday" == "Saturday" is
True)
```

```
# True AND True AND True -> True
if temperature > 25 and not is_raining_now and day_of_week == "Saturday":
    print("It's a warm, dry Saturday! Perfect outdoor weather.")
elif temperature > 25 and not is_raining_now: # Condition: Warm AND not
raining
    print("It's warm and dry, but not the weekend.")
elif temperature > 25 or not is_raining_now: # Condition: Warm OR not raining
(less strict)
        print("It's either warm or not raining (or both).")
else:
    print("Conditions for ideal weather not met.")


print("Weather check finished.")
```

Save and run. Since temperature > 25 is True, not is_raining_now is True, and day_of_week == "Saturday" is True, the first if condition (True and True and True) evaluates to True, and its block is executed. The elif and else are skipped.

Step Explanation: In the first if statement, we chained together three conditions using and. All three individual comparisons/boolean checks (temperature > 25, not is_raining_now, day_of_week == "Saturday") must be True for the *entire* condition to be True.

Order of Operations for Logical Operators: Just like arithmetic operators, logical operators have an order of operations. not is evaluated first, then and, then or. Parentheses () can be used to group conditions and override the default order, making your conditions clearer.

(condition1 and condition2) or condition3: Evaluates the and first, then the or.
condition1 and (condition2 or condition3): Evaluates the or first, then the and.

Example:

```
# decisions.py - Add these examples


print("\n--- Logical Operator Order of Operations ---")


is_admin = True
is_editor = False
is_viewer = True


# Rule: Must be an admin OR (an editor AND a viewer)
```

```
# How would this evaluate? (True or (False and True)) -> (True or False) ->
True
if is_admin or (is_editor and is_viewer):
    print("Allowed access (Admin OR (Editor AND Viewer)).")
else:
    print("Access denied.")


# Rule: Must be an admin AND (an editor OR a viewer)
# How would this evaluate? (True and (False or True)) -> (True and True) ->
True
if is_admin and (is_editor or is_viewer):
    print("Allowed access (Admin AND (Editor OR Viewer)).")
else:
    print("Access denied.")
```

Save and run. See how the parentheses group the conditions and affect the outcome, just like in math. Always use parentheses to make your intentions clear when combining and and or.

Learning to combine conditions using and, or, and not is a fundamental skill that unlocks the ability to make sophisticated decisions in your programs. Instead of just checking one simple thing, you can check multiple criteria simultaneously.

My personal programs became significantly more realistic once I felt comfortable combining conditions. I could implement rules like "grant bonus points if the player finished the level quickly *and* collected all items," or "show a warning if the battery is low *or* the network is disconnected." It makes your code reflect the complexity of the real-world problems you're trying to solve.

You've taken a crucial step in making your programs intelligent! You understand how to combine simpler boolean conditions using the **logical operators and**, **or**, and **not** in Python. You know how these operators work (both true for and, at least one true for or, reverses truth for not) and how to use them directly within your **if** and **elif** statements. You've also seen how the order of operations and parentheses apply to logical combinations.

This ability to build complex boolean expressions is essential for writing programs that can respond accurately to nuanced situations and multiple factors. This, along with repeating actions (loops), forms the backbone of program control flow. Now that we can make programs decide *and* repeat, we have the core tools for controlling the execution path. In the next chapter, we'll look at **loops**, which allow us to repeat actions, building on our knowledge of conditions to decide *how many times* or *how long* to repeat.

5.4 Nested Conditionals

For even more complex decision logic, you can place `if`, `elif`, or `else` statements *inside* the code block of another `if`, `elif`, or `else` statement. This is called **nested conditionals**.

```python
# decisions.py - Add these examples

print("\n--- Nested Conditionals ---")

user_role = "admin"
is_editor = True # This user has editing privileges

if user_role == "admin":
    print("Welcome, Admin!")
    # Nested check: If they are an admin, ARE they also an editor?
    if is_editor:
        print("You have full editing rights.")
    else:
        print("You are an admin, but do not have editing privileges.")
elif user_role == "editor":
    print("Welcome, Editor!")
    # Nested check: If they are an editor, do they have permission?
    if is_editor: # In this scenario, this would likely always be True
        print("You can edit content.")
    else:
        print("You seem to be an editor but lack permission?") # This path
indicates a potential logic issue
else:
    print("Welcome, User.")
    print("You have basic access.")


# Another common pattern: check a main condition, then nested checks inside
item_status = "available"
quantity = 5

if item_status == "available":
    print("Item is in stock.")
    if quantity > 0:
        print(f"There are {quantity} units available.")
```

```
    if quantity < 10: # Another nested check
        print("Low stock warning!")
    else: # Nested else for quantity <= 0
        print("Item is listed as available, but quantity is zero.")
else: # Main else for item_status != "available"
    print("Item is out of stock.")
```

Save and run.

Step Explanation: We have `if` statements inside other `if` or `elif` blocks. The inner conditional is only checked if the outer conditional's block is executed. This allows you to create multi-level decision trees. Correct indentation is absolutely crucial here to keep track of which `if`/`elif`/`else` belongs to which outer block.

Nested conditionals are powerful but can make code harder to read if they get too deep. If you find yourself nesting many levels deep, it might be a sign that the logic could be simplified or broken out into functions.

5.5 Case/Switch Statements (Depending on Language Example)

Some programming languages (like JavaScript, Java, C++) have a `switch` or `case` statement as an alternative way to handle multiple checks against a *single* variable's value.

Python doesn't have a traditional `switch` statement like C++ or Java. The Pythonic way to handle checks against a single value with multiple potential outcomes is usually an `if-elif-else` chain, which is very flexible as the conditions in each `elif` can be completely different if needed. (Note: Python 3.10 introduced `match` statements, which are similar to switch, but `if/elif/else` is the standard for beginners).

So, in Python, for multiple checks against one value, you'll use the `if-elif-else` structure we just covered.

```
# In languages like JavaScript, you might see something like:
/*
let day = "Tuesday";
switch (day) {
    case "Monday":
        console.log("It's Monday");
        break; // IMPORTANT in switch!
    case "Tuesday":
        console.log("It's Tuesday");
        break;
```

```
    default:
        console.log("Some other day");
}
*/


# In Python, the equivalent is usually an if-elif-else chain:
day = "Tuesday"

if day == "Monday":
    print("It's Monday")
elif day == "Tuesday":
    print("It's Tuesday")
else:
    print("Some other day")
```

This reinforces that the *concept* (checking one value against multiple possibilities) is common, but the *syntax* varies.

My personal experience with `switch` statements in other languages is that they are sometimes slightly cleaner than long `if-elif` chains when you are *only* checking for equality against a single variable's value, but the `if-elif-else` chain is more versatile because each `elif` can have a completely different type of condition.

You've unlocked a fundamental power of programming: making decisions! You understand the need for conditional logic and how to implement it using `if`, `elif`, and `else` statements in Python. You know that conditions are boolean expressions and how to combine them using logical operators. You also learned how to create nested conditionals for more complex logic.

The ability to control the flow of your program based on conditions is essential for building programs that can respond to different inputs and situations. This, along with repeating actions (loops), forms the backbone of program control flow. Speaking of repeating actions, that's exactly what we'll cover in the next chapter!

Chapter 6

Control Flow: Repeating Actions

Alright, you can make your program think (decide) based on conditions. That's powerful! But what if you need to perform the same action multiple times? Imagine you have a list of 100 names, and you need to print a personalized greeting for each one. You *could* write `print("Hello, Alice!")`, `print("Hello, Bob!")`, etc., 100 times. That would be incredibly tedious and impractical if the list changes or grows to 1000 names.

This is where the second main type of **control flow** comes in: **repetition**, handled by **loops**. Loops allow a program to execute a block of code repeatedly, either a specific number of times or as long as a certain condition is true.

6.1 The Need for Repetition (Loops)

Repeating tasks is incredibly common in programming.

- Processing every item in a list (like sending an email to every address in a contact list).
- Performing a calculation until a certain result is achieved (like finding the square root of a number).
- Handling user input until valid data is entered.
- Drawing elements on a screen (like each enemy in a game).
- Reading every line of a file.

Loops automate these repetitive tasks, allowing you to write the code for the action *once* and have the computer perform it many times.

My first encounter with loops felt like unlocking automation magic. The idea that I could write code that said "do this thing to *each* item" instead of writing code for *each individual* item was a fundamental shift in how I thought about building programs. It's essential for efficiency and handling collections of data.

There are different types of loops, suited for different situations. The two most common in Python (and many other languages) are `for` loops and `while` loops.

6.2 `for` Loops: Repeating a Specific Number of Times

The `for` loop is typically used when you know in advance how many times you want to repeat something, or when you want to iterate over a sequence of items (like looping through the items in a list or the characters in a string).

In many languages (like C++, Java), `for` loops often have a specific structure involving an initialization step, a condition to check, and an iteration step. Python's `for` loop is slightly different; it's designed to iterate directly over the items of a sequence. However, you can use the built-in `range()` function to easily repeat a block of code a specific number of times, which feels similar to the count-based `for` loops in other languages.

Let's write some `for` loop examples in a new file, `loops.py`.

```python
# loops.py

print("--- FOR Loop (Counting) ---")

# Use range(5) to repeat the loop 5 times (for numbers 0, 1, 2, 3, 4)
for i in range(5):
  # This block will execute 5 times
  print("Iteration number:", i)

print("FOR loop finished.")

print("\n--- FOR Loop (Counting with start and step) ---")

# Use range(start, stop, step)
# Start at 2, stop BEFORE 10, increment by 2
for number in range(2, 10, 2):
    print("Even number:", number) # Output: 2, 4, 6, 8
```

Save and run `python loops.py`.

```
--- FOR Loop (Counting) ---
Iteration number: 0
Iteration number: 1
Iteration number: 2
Iteration number: 3
Iteration number: 4
FOR loop finished.

--- FOR Loop (Counting with start and step) ---
Even number: 2
Even number: 4
Even number: 6
```

```
Even number: 8
```

Step Explanation:

1. `for i in range(5)::` This `for` loop uses `range(5)`. `range(5)` generates a sequence of numbers starting from 0 up to (but not including) 5. So, the numbers are 0, 1, 2, 3, 4.
2. In each repetition (or **iteration**) of the loop, the variable `i` is assigned the *next* value from the sequence (0, then 1, then 2, etc.).
3. The code block indented below the `for` loop (the `print` statement) is executed for each value of `i`.
4. Once all values from `range(5)` have been used, the loop finishes, and the program continues after the indented block.
5. `range(2, 10, 2)` starts at 2, goes up to (but not including) 10, and increments by 2 each time, producing 2, 4, 6, 8.

6.2.1 Looping Through Sequences (Iterating)

A very common and powerful use of `for` loops in Python is iterating directly over the items in a sequence like a list or a string (which are types of data structures, covered more in Chapter 8).

```python
# loops.py - Add these examples

print("\n--- FOR Loop (Iterating over a List) ---")

fruits = ["apple", "banana", "cherry"]

for fruit in fruits:
  # In each iteration, 'fruit' is assigned the next item from the list
  print("Current fruit:", fruit)

print("\n--- FOR Loop (Iterating over a String) ---")

greeting = "Hello"

for character in greeting:
  # In each iteration, 'character' is assigned the next character from the
string
  print("Current character:", character)
```

Save and run.

```
--- FOR Loop (Iterating over a List) ---
Current fruit: apple
Current fruit: banana
Current fruit: cherry


--- FOR Loop (Iterating over a String) ---
Current character: H
Current character: e
Current character: l
Current character: l
Current character: o
```

Step Explanation:

1. `for fruit in fruits:`: This `for` loop directly iterates over the `fruits` list. In the first iteration, `fruit` is assigned the value "apple". In the second, "banana", and so on, until all items in the list are covered.
2. `for character in greeting:`: Similarly, this loop iterates over the `greeting` string, assigning each character ('H', 'e', 'l', 'l', 'o') to the `character` variable in turn.

Using `for` loops to iterate over sequences is incredibly common. It allows you to perform an action (like printing, processing, or modifying) on every single item in a collection of data without knowing exactly how many items there are or accessing them by index number (though you can do that too if needed).

6.3 `while` Loops: Repeating as Long as a Condition is True

The `while` loop is used when you want to repeat a block of code *as long as a certain condition remains True*. You often use a `while` loop when you don't know in advance how many times the loop will need to run.

The structure is simpler than a traditional count-based `for` loop: just the keyword `while`, the condition, and the indented code block.

6.3.1 Loop Structure (Condition, Code Block)

```python
# loops.py - Add these examples


print("\n--- WHILE Loop ---")


count = 0 # Initialize a variable to control the loop
```

```python
while count < 3: # The condition: loop as long as 'count' is less than 3
    # This block is executed in each iteration as long as 'count < 3' is True
    print("Count is:", count)
    count = count + 1 # IMPORTANT: Update the variable used in the condition!

print("WHILE loop finished.")


print("\n--- WHILE Loop Example 2 (User Input Idea) ---")

# Imagine getting user input, you might loop until valid input is given
is_input_valid = False # Start with False

# In a real program, you'd get input here and set is_input_valid based on it
# For this example, we'll simulate it changing
attempts = 0
max_attempts = 3

while not is_input_valid and attempts < max_attempts:
    print(f"Attempt {attempts + 1} to get valid input...")
    # --- Imagine code here tries to get and validate input ---
    # If validation passed, you would set is_input_valid = True
    # For now, we'll just increment attempts
    attempts += 1

    if attempts == max_attempts: # Simulate failure after max attempts
        print("Max attempts reached.")
        # is_input_valid remains False

    # --- End imagination ---


if is_input_valid:
    print("Valid input received!")
else:
    print("Could not get valid input after attempts.")
```

Save and run.

```
--- WHILE Loop ---
Count is: 0
Count is: 1
Count is: 2
WHILE loop finished.

--- WHILE Loop Example 2 (User Input Idea) ---
Attempt 1 to get valid input...
Attempt 2 to get valid input...
Attempt 3 to get valid input...
Max attempts reached.
Could not get valid input after attempts.
```

Step Explanation:

1. `count = 0`: We initialize a variable (`count`) *before* the loop.
2. `while count < 3:`: The condition `count < 3` is checked. Since `0 < 3` is `True`, the loop block executes.
3. Inside the loop, `print("Count is:", count)` executes.
4. `count = count + 1` (or `count += 1`) is crucial! This updates the `count` variable.
5. After the block, the program goes back to the `while` line and checks the condition again (`1 < 3`, which is `True`). The loop executes again.
6. This repeats until `count` becomes 3. The condition `3 < 3` is `False`. The loop finishes, and the program moves on.
7. The second example shows a `while` loop with a more complex condition (`not is_input_valid and attempts < max_attempts`). It loops as long as the input is *not* valid AND we haven't exceeded the maximum number of attempts.

6.3.2 Avoiding Infinite Loops

You understand while loops – they keep repeating a block of code *as long as* a certain condition is True. This is incredibly powerful for situations where you don't know exactly how many repetitions are needed, like waiting for valid user input or processing items until a certain state is reached.

But with that power comes a responsibility: ensuring the loop condition will **eventually become False**. If the condition *never* becomes False, your while loop will run forever, executing the same block of code endlessly. This is called an **infinite loop**.

An infinite loop will cause your program to become unresponsive, consume your computer's resources (CPU, memory), and effectively freeze. You'll typically have to manually force the program to stop (often by pressing Ctrl + C in the terminal).

Think of it like giving someone instructions: "Keep walking forward as long as you are on this street corner." If they are indeed on the street corner, they'll take a step. Then they are *still* on the street corner (unless they step off it). If the instruction doesn't include a way for them to *leave* the street corner or a *limit* on how many steps to take, they'll just walk in place indefinitely.

In programming, an infinite loop usually happens because the code inside the while loop doesn't change the variables or conditions that control whether the loop should continue.

Why Infinite Loops Happen (and How to Avoid Them)

The structure of a while loop is:

```
# Conceptual WHILE loop structure

# Initialize variables used in the condition (if any)
variable_controlling_loop = initial_value

# WHILE the condition is True:
while variable_controlling_loop meets some criteria:
    # --- Loop Body ---
    # Do some task(s)
    # ...

    # CRITICAL STEP: Update the variable(s) used in the condition!
    variable_controlling_loop = new_value_based_on_task
    # Or update other variables used in the condition

    # Or include a way to break out (using 'break', covered in 6.5)
    # if some_other_condition_met:
    #     break
    # --- End Loop Body ---

# Code after the loop
```

The most common cause of an infinite loop is **forgetting or failing to update the variable(s) that the loop condition depends on** within the loop body.

Let's look at an example of what *not* to do (and how to fix it):

```
# infinite_loop_danger.py
```

```
# DANGEROUS EXAMPLE - WILL CAUSE AN INFINITE LOOP!
# Comment this out or be ready to press Ctrl + C to stop it.

# count = 0
#
# while count < 5:
#     print("This loop will run forever!")
#     # MISSING: There is no code here to change the value of 'count'
#     # So, if count starts at 0, 0 < 5 is always True!

print("This line will not be reached by the infinite loop.") # This line
won't print if the loop is infinite
```

Step Explanation: The count variable starts at 0. The condition count < 5 is True. The loop body prints the message. Then the program returns to the while line. The condition count < 5 is *still* True because count is still 0. This repeats endlessly.

How to Fix It: You must include a line inside the loop that changes the value of count in a way that will eventually make the condition count < 5 false.

```
# infinite_loop_fixed.py

print("--- Fixing an Infinite Loop ---")

count = 0

while count < 5:
    print("This loop runs correctly.", count)
    # ADDED: Update the variable controlling the loop
    count += 1 # Increase count by 1 in each iteration

print("Loop finished successfully.")
```

Save and run python infinite_loop_fixed.py.

```
--- Fixing an Infinite Loop ---
This loop runs correctly. 0
This loop runs correctly. 1
This loop runs correctly. 2
This loop runs correctly. 3
```

```
This loop runs correctly. 4
Loop finished successfully.
```

Step Explanation: Now, the count += 1 line inside the loop increments count in each iteration. After 5 iterations, count becomes 5. The condition count < 5 (which is 5 < 5) becomes False. The loop terminates correctly, and the program continues after the loop block.

My personal experience with infinite loops usually involved subtly forgetting to update a condition variable, or having a complex condition where I didn't think through all the possible ways it could *fail* to become false. For example, in a loop that processes items from a list, if I wasn't removing the items or moving to the next one correctly, the "while list is not empty" condition would never become false.

Common Scenarios and Checks:
- **Counting Loops:** If your while loop is meant to count up or down, ensure you are incrementing or decrementing the counter variable *in every iteration*.
- **Processing Item Loops:** If your while loop processes items (e.g., from a list or database query), ensure that in each iteration, you are either removing the processed item or advancing to the *next* unprocessed item, so the "are there more items?" condition eventually becomes false.
- **User Input Loops:** If you're looping until valid input is given (while input is invalid), ensure you are prompting the user and *getting new input* inside the loop, and that there is logic to check the new input's validity and set a boolean flag or variable appropriately to eventually make the loop condition false.
- **Break Conditions:** As we saw in Section 6.5, you can also design a while True: loop (a loop that would run forever if not stopped) but include an if statement inside with a break keyword to exit the loop when a specific condition is met. This is an explicit way to ensure termination.

```python
# loops.py - Example using while True with break (Add to file)

print("\n--- WHILE True with BREAK ---")

# This loop will run until the user types 'quit'

while True: # This condition is always True, so the loop would be infinite
without a break
    command = input("Enter a command (or 'quit' to exit): ")
    if command == 'quit': # Check the condition to exit
        print("Exiting loop.")
        break # Exit the loop immediately
```

```
# If we didn't break, process the command
print(f"Executing command: {command}")

print("Program finished after loop break.")
```

Save and run. Type different things, then type quit. This shows how break can be used to terminate a loop whose continuation condition might be complex or depends on user action.

Learning to spot potential infinite loop scenarios in your while loops is a critical skill. Always ask yourself: "Is there definitely something in this loop's body that will eventually make the while condition false?"

You've tackled a fundamental challenge in loop programming: avoiding infinite loops. You now understand what an infinite loop is, why it happens (usually due to a condition that never becomes false), and how to prevent it by ensuring you update the variables controlling the loop within the loop's body, or by using explicit break statements.

Being mindful of loop termination conditions is essential for writing reliable programs that don't freeze or crash. This skill, combined with your knowledge of loops and conditions, solidifies your understanding of program control flow. In the next chapter, we'll look at **functions**, which help us organize these complex control flow structures into reusable blocks.

6.4 do...while Loops

Alright, you've learned about for loops (good for iterating a known number of times or over sequences) and while loops (good for repeating as long as a condition is true, checking *before* each repetition). Now, let's talk about a loop variation you'll encounter if you learn other languages, called a do...while loop.

The key characteristic of a **do...while loop** is that its condition is checked *after* the loop body has executed. This means the code inside the do...while loop is guaranteed to run **at least once**, regardless of whether the condition is initially true or false. After the first execution, it checks the condition and continues looping as long as the condition is true.

Think about an instruction like: "Take a step forward. *Then*, if you are not yet at the door, take another step forward, and keep doing this until you reach the door." The very first step is taken regardless of your starting position relative to the door. Only subsequent steps depend on the condition.

This contrasts with a standard while loop, where the condition is checked *before* the first iteration. If the condition is initially false, a while loop's body will never execute at all.

```python
# Standard WHILE loop behavior (Python)

print("--- WHILE loop ---")

x = 10 # Variable for the condition
# Condition: x < 5 (This is initially False)
while x < 5:
    # This print statement will never run because the condition is checked
first
    print("This is inside the WHILE loop.")
    x += 1 # This line is never reached

print("Finished the WHILE loop.")
# Output:
# --- WHILE loop ---
# Finished the WHILE loop.
```

Commentary: See how the code inside the while block was completely skipped because the condition was false from the start? That's standard while loop behavior.

Now, let's *conceptually* imagine a do...while loop structure (remembering this specific syntax doesn't exist in Python):

```python
# CONCEPTUAL DO-WHILE loop structure (Not actual Python syntax!)

# Initialize variable (maybe needed in the loop body or condition)
# variable_for_condition = initial_value

# DO: (Execute this block AT LEAST ONCE)
# do {
#     # --- Loop Body ---
#     # Perform some task(s)
#     # ...
#
#     # Update variable(s) used in the condition!
#     # variable_for_condition = new_value
#     # --- End Loop Body ---
# } WHILE (variable_for_condition meets some criteria); # Check condition
AFTER the body
# End DO-WHILE
```

Use Cases Where do...while is Natural:

do...while is particularly useful in situations where you need to:

- Get input from a user and then validate it, repeating the process *only if* the input is invalid. You need to *ask* for input at least once.
- Execute a task at least once before checking if it needs to be repeated.

For example, in languages that have do...while, getting guaranteed valid user input often looks like this:

```
// Example using JavaScript's do...while loop (conceptual, not Python)

/*
let userInput; // Variable to store input

do {
    userInput = prompt("Please enter a number greater than 10:"); // Get
input (happens at least once)
    // Assume prompt returns a string
    // And assume there's validation logic here (e.g., checking if it's a
number and > 10)
    var isValid = !isNaN(userInput) && parseInt(userInput) > 10; // Basic
validation example
    if (!isValid) {
        alert("Invalid input. Please try again.");
    }
} while (!isValid); // Repeat AS LONG AS the input is NOT valid

console.log("Valid input received:", userInput);
*/
```

Commentary: The code inside the do { ... } block (prompting for input, basic validation) runs the first time. *Then* the while (!isValid) condition is checked. If isValid is False (because the user entered invalid input), the loop repeats. This continues until isValid becomes True. The key is that the prompt instruction runs at least once.

How to Achieve do...while Behavior in Python

Since Python doesn't have a native do...while loop, how do you achieve the same behavior (guaranteeing the loop body runs at least once)?

You have a couple of common options in Python:

1. **Repeat the code block before the while loop:** Write the code you want to run at least once before the loop, then use a standard while loop for subsequent iterations based on the condition.

```
2.  # do_while_in_python_option1.py
3.
4.  print("--- DO-WHILE in Python (Option 1) ---")
5.
6.  # Repeat the code block once initially
7.  user_input = input("Enter something: ")
8.  # Check the condition based on the first input
9.  is_valid = (user_input != "") # Example: is it not empty?
10.
11.  # Now use a standard WHILE loop for subsequent tries
12.  while not is_valid: # While the input is NOT valid
13.      print("Input cannot be empty. Please try again.")
14.      user_input = input("Enter something: ") # Get input again inside
    the loop
15.      is_valid = (user_input != "") # Re-check the condition
16.

    print(f"Valid input received: '{user_input}'")
```

Step Explanation: We explicitly call input() and check is_valid once before the while loop. The while loop then only runs if is_valid is False, repeatedly asking for input and checking the condition until it becomes True.

17. **Use a while True loop with a break statement:** Create an infinite loop (while True:) and use an if statement with a break keyword inside the loop to exit when the desired condition for *stopping* the loop is met.

```
18.  # do_while_in_python_option2.py
19.
20.  print("\n--- DO-WHILE in Python (Option 2 - WHILE True with BREAK) ---
    ")
21.
22.  while True: # This loop runs indefinitely unless broken
23.      user_input = input("Enter a number greater than 10: ") # Get input
    (runs at least once)
24.
25.      # Check if the input is valid (our condition)
26.      try:
```

```
27.          number = int(user_input)
28.          if number > 10:
29.              is_valid = True
30.          else:
31.              is_valid = False
32.              print("Number must be greater than 10.")
33.      except ValueError:
34.          is_valid = False
35.          print("Invalid input. Please enter a whole number.")
36.
37.      if is_valid:
38.          break # If the input IS valid, break out of the WHILE True
     loop
39.
40.      # If we didn't break, the loop continues (because is_valid was
     False)
41.
     print(f"Valid input received: {number}")
```

Step Explanation: The while True: guarantees the code block runs at least once. Inside the loop, we get input, validate it, and set an is_valid flag. The if is_valid: check then determines if the break statement is executed. If is_valid is True, break exits the loop. If is_valid is False, break is skipped, and the while True: condition remains True, so the loop repeats. This effectively achieves the do...while behavior.

My personal preference is often the while True with break approach (Option 2), especially for input validation loops. It feels a bit cleaner as the input and validation logic are entirely contained within the loop block, even for the first attempt.

Understanding the do...while loop's characteristic (condition checked *after*) is important if you learn other languages. Knowing how to replicate that behavior using standard while loops and break statements in Python ensures you can handle those "run at least once" scenarios effectively.

You've learned about a loop structure, the do...while loop, that's common elsewhere, understanding its key difference from a standard while loop (guaranteed execution at least once). You also learned how to achieve the same "run at least once" behavior in Python using two common patterns: repeating code before a while loop, or using a while True loop with a break statement triggered by your condition.

While Python doesn't have this specific syntax, the concept is important, and you now know how to implement the required control flow using the tools Python provides. This solidifies your understanding of different loop structures and how to choose or implement the right one for the job. This completes our look at fundamental control flow!

6.5 Controlling Loop Execution (Break and Continue)

Sometimes, you might want to alter the standard flow of a loop while it's running. The `break` and `continue` statements allow you to do this.

```python
# loops.py - Add these examples

print("\n--- Loop Control: BREAK ---")

# Use break to exit a loop early

count = 0
while count < 10: # This loop *could* run up to 10 times
    print("Checking count:", count)
    if count == 5: # If count reaches 5
        print("Count is 5, breaking out of the loop!")
        break # Exit the WHILE loop immediately
    count += 1 # Update count

print("Loop broken. Code continues here.")


print("\n--- Loop Control: CONTINUE ---")

# Use continue to skip the rest of the current iteration and go to the next
one

numbers = [1, 2, 3, 4, 5, 6, 7, 8, 9, 10]

for number in numbers:
    # Check if the number is odd
    if number % 2 != 0: # If the remainder when divided by 2 is NOT 0
        print(f"Skipping odd number: {number}")
        continue # Skip the rest of this iteration, go to the next number in
the list
```

```
        # This line only executes if the number was NOT odd (i.e., was even)
        print(f"Processing even number: {number}")


print("Finished processing numbers.")
```

Save and run.

```
--- Loop Control: BREAK ---
Checking count: 0
Checking count: 1
Checking count: 2
Checking count: 3
Checking count: 4
Checking count: 5
Count is 5, breaking out of the loop!
Loop broken. Code continues here.

--- Loop Control: CONTINUE ---
Skipping odd number: 1
Processing even number: 2
Skipping odd number: 3
Processing even number: 4
Skipping odd number: 5
Processing even number: 6
Skipping odd number: 7
Processing even number: 8
Skipping odd number: 9
Processing even number: 10
Finished processing numbers.
```

Step Explanation:

1. break: When count hits 5, the if count == 5: condition becomes True.
    The print statement runs, and then break is encountered. break immediately stops the
    execution of the innermost loop it is in. The program jumps out of the while loop and
    continues with the line print("Loop broken...").
2. continue: In the for loop, when number is odd (1, 3, 5, etc.), the if number % 2 !=
    0: condition is True. The "Skipping odd number" message is printed, and then continue is
    encountered. continue immediately stops the *current iteration* of the loop and jumps to
    the *next iteration*. For the for loop iterating over a list, this means moving to the next item in

the list. The `print(f"Processing even number: {number}")` line is skipped for odd numbers. For even numbers, the `if` condition is `False`, so the `continue` is skipped, and the "Processing even number" line is executed.

`break` is useful for exiting a loop when a certain condition is met, even if the loop's main condition or sequence hasn't finished. `continue` is useful for skipping processing for specific items or situations within a loop iteration and moving directly to the next one.

You've now added the second essential pillar of control flow: repetition! You understand the need for loops and how to use **for loops** for iterating over sequences or repeating a fixed number of times, and **while loops** for repeating as long as a condition remains true. You've learned the critical importance of avoiding **infinite loops** in `while` loops and how to use `break` and `continue` to control loop execution flow.

Loops are incredibly powerful for automating tasks and processing collections of data. Along with conditional statements (Chapter 5), they give your programs the ability to adapt and handle dynamic situations.

With decision making and repetition covered, you have the core tools to control the flow of your program's execution. In the next chapter, we'll look at **functions**, which allow us to organize our code into reusable blocks, making our programs more modular and easier to manage.

Chapter 7
Functions: Building Blocks of Code

Alright, you can store data, perform calculations, make decisions, and repeat actions. You're building logical programs! But imagine writing a complex program, like a user registration system. You might need to validate an email address in several places: when the user signs up, when they update their profile, maybe when you import a list of users. Copying and pasting the same email validation code everywhere would be tedious and error-prone. What if you need to change the validation rule later? You'd have to find and update every copy of that code!

This is the problem that **functions** solve.

7.1 What is a Function?

A **function** is a named, reusable block of code that performs a specific task. You can define a function once and then "call" or "invoke" it from anywhere else in your program to execute the code inside it.

Think of a function like a mini-program or a specialized tool. You give it a name (like validate_email or calculate_total), it might take some specific inputs (like the email address to validate), it performs its task (checks the format), and it might produce an output (like True or False indicating if the email is valid).

7.1.1 Why Use Functions? (Reusability, Organization)

Using functions offers several key benefits:

- **Reusability:** Write a block of code once, and use it whenever you need that task performed. This avoids repetition and makes your code much shorter and more efficient.
- **Organization:** Break down a large program into smaller, logical pieces. Each function handles one specific task, making the overall program easier to read, understand, and manage.
- **Readability:** Giving a block of code a descriptive name (calculate_shipping_cost) makes the main part of your program easier to follow than reading the raw code for that calculation every time it appears.
- **Maintainability:** If you need to change how a task is performed (e.g., update the shipping cost calculation logic), you only need to modify the code in *one* place – inside the function definition. All parts of your program that *call* that function will automatically use the updated logic.
- **Testability:** You can test individual functions independently to ensure they perform their specific task correctly, which makes debugging easier.

Functions are absolutely fundamental to writing well-structured, maintainable, and efficient software. They are one of the most important concepts you will learn.

My personal transition to using functions felt like going from writing a single, long instruction manual to creating a manual that references other, more specific mini-manuals for common procedures. The main manual became much shorter and easier to follow, and I could update the mini-manuals without rewriting the whole thing.

7.2 Defining a Function

Alright, you know *why* functions are awesome (reusability, organization!). Now, let's learn how to make one. Defining a function is like writing down that mini-manual for a specific procedure, giving it a title, and maybe noting any specific information the procedure needs.

In Python, defining a function involves using the keyword **def** (short for "define").

The basic syntax for defining a function looks like this:

```
def function_name(parameter1, parameter2, ...):
    # This is the function body
    # Code that the function executes goes here
    # This block is indented
    # ...
    # Optionally, use the 'return' keyword to send a result back
    # return some_value
```

Let's break this down and create some simple functions in a new file, function_definition.py.

```
# function_definition.py

print("--- Function Definition ---")

# 1. Define a simple function with no parameters
# 'def' keyword, function name 'say_hello', empty parentheses ()
def say_hello():
    # This is the function body - remember the indentation!
    print("Hello there!")
    print("Nice to see you.")

# 2. Define a function that takes one parameter
# Parameter 'name' is listed inside the parentheses
```

```python
def greet_person(name):
    # The parameter 'name' is available as a variable inside the function
body
    print(f"Hello, {name}!")


# 3. Define a function that takes multiple parameters
# Parameters 'num1' and 'num2' are listed inside the parentheses, separated
by commas
def add_numbers(num1, num2):
    sum_result = num1 + num2
    # This function doesn't return a value yet, it just calculates and stores
sum_result
    # We'll learn about returning values in 7.4
    print(f"The sum of {num1} and {num2} is {sum_result}")


# 4. Define a function with no parameters that performs a task
def show_instructions():
    print("--- Instructions ---")
    print("Step 1: Do this.")
    print("Step 2: Do that.")
    print("-------------------")



# Note: Defining these functions does NOT execute the code inside them!
# Running this script now will only print the "--- Function Definition ---"
line.
# We need to CALL the functions to run their code (covered in 7.3).


print("Finished defining functions.")
```

Save the file. If you run python function_definition.py, you'll see:

```
--- Function Definition ---
Finished defining functions.
```

Step Explanation:

1. def say_hello():: We use the def keyword followed by the function name say_hello. The
   empty parentheses () indicate that this function doesn't require any specific inputs
   (parameters) to run. The colon : is required after the parentheses.

2. The lines print("Hello there!") and print("Nice to see you.") are the function body. They are **indented** to show they belong to this function. Any code at this level of indentation is part of the say_hello function. When the indentation goes back to the level of def, the function definition is finished.

3. def greet_person(name):: This function is named greet_person. The parentheses () contain name. name is a **parameter** – a placeholder variable that will hold the value passed *into* the function when it's called. Inside the function, name behaves like any other variable.

4. def add_numbers(num1, num2):: This function named add_numbers takes two parameters, num1 and num2. These parameters are separated by commas.

5. The code inside add_numbers uses the parameter variables (num1, num2) to perform a calculation.

Function Name:

- Follow the same rules as variable names (start with letter or underscore, contain only letters, numbers, underscores).
- Follow the same naming conventions: use descriptive names that indicate what the function *does* (e.g., calculate_area, send_email, process_user_data).
- In Python, the convention is to use snake_case for function names (say_hello, greet_person, add_numbers).

Parameters (Inputs):

- Parameters are listed inside the parentheses () in the function definition.
- They act as variables *local* to the function (Section 7.5). When you call the function, the values you provide as arguments are assigned to these parameter variables.
- If a function doesn't need any inputs, you leave the parentheses empty (()).
- If it needs multiple inputs, list parameter names separated by commas.
- The order of parameters matters when you call the function (arguments are matched by position to parameters, by default).

The Function Body (Code to Execute):

- This is the indented block of code immediately following the def line and the colon :.
- This is the sequence of instructions that the function performs when it is called.
- The function body can contain any valid Python code: variable assignments, operators, conditional statements (if/else), loops (for/while), calls to other functions, etc.

My personal experience here highlights that sometimes, especially with functions that take multiple parameters, thinking carefully about the *order* of parameters and using clear names makes calling the function later much less error-prone. If a function takes width and height, def calculate_area(width, height): is clearer than def calculate_area(a, b):.

Defining the function sets it up, but remember the code inside it won't run until you explicitly **call** the function, which is the next step!

You've now learned how to **define a function** in Python using the def keyword. You understand that a function has a name, can accept inputs via **parameters** listed in parentheses, and contains a block of indented code (the function body) that executes when the function is called. You also know that just defining a function doesn't run its code.

This ability to define reusable blocks of code is a major step towards writing organized and efficient programs. In the next section (7.3), we'll learn how to actually **call** these functions to make their code execute.

7.3 Calling a Function

To execute the code inside a function, you need to **call** or **invoke** it. You do this by writing the function's name followed by parentheses ().

```python
# functions.py - Add to the bottom of the file

print("\n--- Calling a Function ---")

greet()  # Call the greet function
greet()  # Call the greet function again

print("Function calls finished.")
```

Save and run python functions.py.

```
--- Function Definition ---

--- Calling a Function ---
Hello!
Welcome!
Hello!
Welcome!
Function calls finished.
```

Step Explanation:

1. The program starts and reads the function definition using def greet():. It now knows what greet() means.
2. It encounters print("\n--- Calling a Function ---") and executes it.
3. It encounters the first greet(). This is a function call. The program jumps to the code block defined by the greet function and executes the lines inside it ("Hello!", "Welcome!").
4. After the greet function's block finishes, the program returns to where the function was called and continues with the next line.
5. It encounters the second greet() and executes the function's block again.
6. After the second call finishes, the program continues with print("Function calls finished.").

This shows the reusability! We defined the "Hello! Welcome!" sequence once and ran it twice just by calling the function name.

7.3.1 Passing Arguments (Inputs)

Functions aren't limited to doing the exact same thing every time. They can accept **inputs**, which allow you to give them different information to work with each time you call them. These inputs are specified as **parameters** in the function definition and passed as **arguments** when you call the function.

```python
# functions.py - Add these examples

print("\n--- Passing Arguments ---")

# Define a function that takes one parameter: name
def greet_person(name): # 'name' is the parameter
    print(f"Hello, {name}!") # Use the 'name' parameter in the function body
    print("Welcome!")

# Call the function and pass different arguments
greet_person("Alice") # "Alice" is the argument for the 'name' parameter
greet_person("Bob")   # "Bob" is the argument for the 'name' parameter

print("\n--- Passing Multiple Arguments ---")

# Define a function that takes two parameters: item and price
def display_item_price(item, price):
    print(f"Item: {item}, Price: ${price}")

# Call the function with two arguments
```

```
display_item_price("Laptop", 1200) # "Laptop" for 'item', 1200 for 'price'
display_item_price("Mouse", 25.50) # "Mouse" for 'item', 25.50 for 'price'
```

Save and run.

```
--- Passing Arguments ---
Hello, Alice!
Welcome!
Hello, Bob!
Welcome!


--- Passing Multiple Arguments ---
Item: Laptop, Price: $1200
Item: Mouse, Price: $25.50
```

Step Explanation:

1. def greet_person(name):: We define the function greet_person and specify that it expects one input, which will be referred to by the variable name name *inside* the function.
2. greet_person("Alice"): When we call greet_person, we put "Alice" inside the parentheses. This string "Alice" is passed as the **argument** for the name parameter. Inside the function, the variable name will have the value "Alice".
3. When called with "Bob", the name variable inside the function will have the value "Bob".
4. def display_item_price(item, price):: This function expects two parameters, item and price, in that order.
5. display_item_price("Laptop", 1200): When called, "Laptop" is the argument for the first parameter (item), and 1200 is the argument for the second parameter (price). The arguments are matched to parameters by their position.

Arguments are how you provide dynamic information to your functions, allowing them to perform the same task on different data.

7.4 Returning Values (Outputs)

Besides performing a task, functions can also produce a result or an **output** and send that result back to the part of the program that called the function. This is done using the **return** keyword.

```
# functions.py - Add these examples


print("\n--- Returning Values ---")
```

```python
# Define a function that takes two numbers and returns their sum
def add_numbers(num1, num2):
    sum_result = num1 + num2
    return sum_result # Return the value of sum_result

# Call the function and store the returned value in a variable
total = add_numbers(5, 3) # The function executes, returns 8, and 8 is stored
in 'total'
print("The sum is:", total) # Output: The sum is: 8

# Call the function and print the returned value directly
print("The sum of 10 and 20 is:", add_numbers(10, 20)) # Output: The sum of
10 and 20 is: 30


print("\n--- Returning Different Types ---")

# Function that returns a boolean
def is_even(number):
    if number % 2 == 0:
        return True
    else:
        return False

print("Is 4 even?", is_even(4)) # Output: Is 4 even? True
print("Is 7 even?", is_even(7)) # Output: Is 7 even? False


# Function that returns a string based on input
def get_greeting(hour_of_day):
    if hour_of_day < 12:
        return "Good morning!"
    elif hour_of_day < 18:
        return "Good afternoon!"
    else:
        return "Good evening!"

message = get_greeting(14) # Call the function, return value "Good
afternoon!" is stored in 'message'
```

```
print(message) # Output: Good afternoon!
```

Save and run.

Step Explanation:

1. def add_numbers(num1, num2): ... return sum_result: The function calculates the sum and then uses return sum_result to send that calculated value back to wherever the function was called.
2. total = add_numbers(5, 3): We call add_numbers(5, 3). The function runs, calculates 5 + 3 = 8. The return 8 statement sends the value 8 back. The = operator then assigns this returned value (8) to the variable total.
3. print("...", add_numbers(10, 20)): Here, we call the function directly inside the print statement. The function returns 30, and the print statement then prints that returned value.
4. The is_even function returns boolean values (True or False).
5. The get_greeting function takes a number (hour) and returns a string based on conditional checks.

Functions can return any data type – numbers, strings, booleans, lists, objects, or even nothing (return without a value, or if no return statement is reached, Python functions implicitly return None). The return statement also immediately exits the function. Any code in the function after a return statement will not be executed.

7.5 Scope: Where Variables Live

Variables created inside a function are **local** to that function. They only exist while the function is executing, and they can only be accessed from *within* that function. This is called **local scope**.

Variables created outside of any function (at the main level of your script) have **global scope**. They can be accessed from anywhere in your program, including inside functions.

```
# functions.py - Add these examples

print("\n--- Variable Scope ---")

global_variable = "I am global" # This variable has global scope

def my_function():
    local_variable = "I am local to my_function" # This variable has local scope

    print(global_variable) # Can access global variables
```

```
    print(local_variable)  # Can access local variables

def another_function():
    # print(local_variable) # This would cause an error! local_variable is
not defined in this scope
    print(global_variable) # Can access global variables

my_function()
another_function()

# print(local_variable) # This would also cause an error! Cannot access local
variables outside the function they are defined in.
print("Outside functions:", global_variable)
```

Save and run.

```
--- Variable Scope ---
I am global
I am local to my_function
I am global
Outside functions: I am global
```

Step Explanation:

1. global_variable is defined outside any function, so it's accessible everywhere.
2. my_function can access both global_variable (because it's global)
   and local_variable (because it's defined within my_function's scope).
3. another_function can
   access global_variable but *cannot* access local_variable because local_variable only
   exists inside my_function.
4. Attempting to access local_variable outside of my_function's definition would result in
   a NameError (variable not defined).

Understanding scope is important to know where variables are accessible and to avoid accidental
conflicts between variables with the same name in different parts of your code. Generally, it's best
practice to use local variables within functions and pass data in/out using parameters
and return values rather than relying heavily on modifying global variables from inside functions.

7.6 Function Design Considerations

Alright, you can define and call functions! That's awesome. You can wrap code in a named block, send it some data, and get a result back. But just because you *can* put code in a function doesn't mean you should put *any* code into *any* function. Writing good functions is a craft, and thinking about how you design them will make your programs much better.

As you start using functions in your own code, keep these considerations in mind. They are guidelines, not strict rules, but they represent best practices that experienced programmers follow to write cleaner, more maintainable, and less error-prone code.

My personal journey with function design involved learning that functions weren't just about avoiding repetition; they were about clarity and managing complexity. Initially, I'd write a function that did five different things, and it was hard to understand and even harder to debug if one part failed. Breaking that into five smaller functions, each doing *one* specific thing, made everything so much clearer. It's like organizing a toolbox – each tool has a specific purpose.

Single Responsibility:

What it means: Ideally, a function should perform one specific task and one task only. It should have a single reason to change.
Why it's important:
* **Readability:** A function that does one thing has a name that clearly reflects that task (e.g., calculate_tax, send_confirmation_email, format_phone_number). This makes your code much easier to understand.
* **Testability:** It's much easier to write tests (Chapter 10) for a function that has a single, well-defined input and output than for a function that does multiple things.
* **Reusability:** A function that does one specific task is much more likely to be reusable in different parts of your current program or even in future projects than a function that does many things tied to a specific context.

Example (Illustrative):

```
# Bad Example (Doing too much) - Conceptual
# def process_user_data_and_send_email(user_info):
#       # Validate user info (Task 1)
#       # Save user to database (Task 2)
#       # Generate email content (Task 3)
#       # Send email (Task 4)
#       # Return success status (Task 5)
#       pass # ... implementation details ...
```

```
# Good Example (Single Responsibility) - Conceptual
# def validate_user_info(user_info): # Task 1
#     # ... validation logic ...
#     return is_valid, validation_errors
#
# def save_user(user_data): # Task 2
#     # ... database save logic ...
#     return saved_user_object
#
# def generate_email_content(user_object): # Task 3
#     # ... email content logic ...
#     return email_body
#
# def send_email(recipient, subject, body): # Task 4
#     # ... email sending logic ...
#     return success_status

# Now, your main logic calls these smaller functions:
# user_data = get_user_input()
# is_valid, errors = validate_user_info(user_data)
# if is_valid:
#     saved_user = save_user(user_data)
#     email_body = generate_email_content(saved_user)
#     email_sent = send_email(saved_data.email, "Welcome", email_body)
#     # ... handle results ...
```

Commentary: The second example is much clearer. Each function has one job. You can reuse validate_user_info if you get user data from a different source. You can reuse send_email for other types of emails. If there's a bug in saving to the database, you know exactly which function to look in.

Aim for functions that are relatively short and focused on a single, well-defined task.

Descriptive Names:

What it means: Give your functions names that clearly indicate what they *do*.
Why it's important: Readability! When someone (including your future self) reads your code, they should be able to understand the purpose of a function just by its name, without having to read the code inside it immediately.
Example:

- def calc(a, b): - Bad name, parameters are also unhelpful.
- def calculate_sum(num1, num2): - Good name, clear parameters.
- def process_data(): - Okay, but could be better. What kind of data? What process?
- def format_user_address(address_object): - Much clearer.

Use action verbs in your function names
(e.g., get, calculate, validate, send, draw, process, check).

Clear Parameters:

What it means: Choose parameter names that clearly indicate the type of input the function expects and its role within the function.
Why it's important: When you call a function, seeing display_product_details(name, price, stock) is much more understandable than display_product_details(a, b, c). Clear parameter names also serve as informal documentation for the function's inputs.
Example:

- def create_file(path, content): - Clear.
- def send_message(recipient, subject, body): - Clear.
- def process_list(my_list): - Okay, but maybe data_list or items_to_process is better depending on context.

Return Values:

What it means: If a function computes or produces a result that needs to be used elsewhere in the program, use the return keyword to send that result back.
Why it's important: Functions should ideally communicate with the rest of the program using inputs (parameters) and outputs (return values). Avoid having functions rely heavily on modifying global variables as a way of communicating results; this makes code harder to track and can lead to unexpected side effects.
Example:

```
# Bad Example (Modifying global variable) - Conceptual
# total_count = 0
#
# def add_to_total(value):
#     global total_count # Need global keyword to modify global variable
#     total_count += value
#
# add_to_total(10)
# add_to_total(5)
```

```
# print(total_count) # Works, but relies on global state


# Good Example (Using return) - Conceptual
def calculate_sum_of_two_numbers(num1, num2):
    return num1 + num2 # Return the sum


# Main logic uses the return value:
# current_total = 0
# value1 = calculate_sum_of_two_numbers(10, 5)
# current_total += value1
# value2 = calculate_sum_of_two_numbers(20, 3)
# current_total += value2
# print(current_total) # Easier to track and less side effects
```

Commentary: While modifying global variables is sometimes necessary, relying on return values for a function's primary output makes the function's behavior clearer and its interaction with the rest of the program more explicit.

Avoid Side Effects (When Possible):

What it means: A **side effect** is when a function does something other than just calculating and returning a value. Examples include printing to the console, modifying a global variable, writing to a file, making a network request, or changing the state of an object passed as a parameter (if the language allows).

Why it's important: Functions without side effects (called "pure functions" in some paradigms) are easier to reason about, test, and understand because their output depends *only* on their inputs, and they don't change anything outside themselves. While many functions *must* have side effects (like a function that saves to a database or prints output), try to minimize unnecessary side effects and make them obvious (e.g., a function named print_report clearly has a side effect).

Example: A function named get_formatted_address(address_parts) that returns a nicely formatted string is "purer" than a function named format_and_print_address(address_parts) that both formats the address and prints it directly. The first function is more reusable.

Function Size:

What it means: There's no strict rule, but if a function is getting very long (dozens or hundreds of lines), it might be doing too much (violating the single responsibility principle) or handling too much complexity.

Why it's important: Long functions are harder to read, understand, debug, and test. Breaking them down into smaller, focused functions improves clarity.

My personal process now often involves writing a rough block of code first, getting it working, and *then* looking at it and thinking, "Okay, what specific tasks is this block doing?" Then I'll wrap those tasks into functions with descriptive names and clear parameters/return values. This refactoring step is crucial for transforming working-but-messy code into clean, well-designed code.

Thinking about these considerations as you design your functions will help you write code that is not just functional, but also clean, maintainable, and easy for others (and your future self) to work with.

You've gone beyond just using functions and are now thinking about how to **design** them effectively! You understand the principles of **single responsibility**, using **descriptive names** for functions and parameters, the importance of using **return values** for output, and the concept of **side effects**. You also have guidelines for function size.

Applying these design considerations will significantly improve the quality of your code as your programs grow. This skill, combined with your understanding of core programming concepts, puts you in a great position to write well-structured software. Next, we'll look at **data structures** for organizing collections of data.

Chapter 8
Organizing Collections of Data

Alright! You're building programs that can make decisions, repeat actions, and use functions for reusable logic. That's a solid programming foundation! But imagine keeping track of all the users registered on a website, or all the items in a customer's shopping cart, or all the temperatures recorded over a week. Storing each piece of data in a separate variable would be incredibly cumbersome and impractical.

```
user1 = "Alice"
user2 = "Bob"
user3 = "Charlie"
...
```

How would you loop through those? How would you find a specific user? This is where we need ways to organize collections of data.

This is the purpose of **Data Structures**. A data structure is a particular way of organizing data in a computer so that it can be used efficiently. They provide ways to store multiple values under a single name and access, add, remove, or modify those values in structured ways.

Think about organizing physical items. If you have a list of chores, you might write them on a numbered list (like an ordered sequence). If you have a contact book, you organize it by names, where each name has associated details like phone number and email (like key-value pairs). These are real-world data structures. Programming data structures are similar concepts for organizing data in memory.

My personal journey learning data structures felt like getting new types of containers for my data. Before, everything was just loose variables. Learning about lists and dictionaries provided powerful new ways to manage groups of related information and perform actions on them collectively.

While computer science courses delve deep into many complex data structures, for a beginner, two fundamental ones are crucial: ordered sequences (like Lists or Arrays) and key-value pairs (like Dictionaries or Objects). We'll focus on the most common Python examples here.

8.1 The Need for Data Structures

Alright, you know about variables. You can do `user_name = "Alice"` or `user_age = 30`. But what if you need to keep track of the names and ages of *ten* users? You *could* create ten pairs of variables:

```
user_name_1 = "Alice"
user_age_1 = 30
```

```
user_name_2 = "Bob"
user_age_2 = 25
...
user_name_10 = "Zack"
user_age_10 = 40
```

Now, imagine you need to print the name and age of *every* user. You'd have to write `print()` statements ten times, each referencing a different variable name. What if you needed to calculate the average age of all users? You'd have to add up ten separate age variables and divide by 10. What if you had 100 users? Or 1000? This approach quickly becomes impossible to manage.

This is the fundamental problem that **data structures** solve. A data structure is a way of organizing and storing a collection of data in a computer's memory so that you can work with it efficiently. Instead of using separate variables for each individual piece of data, you use a data structure to group related data together under a single variable name.

Think about organizing information in the real world:

- If you have a shopping list, you use a **list** or **bullet points** – an ordered sequence of items.
- If you have contact information for a friend, you might use a **card** with labeled fields for "Name", "Phone", "Email" – you access the information using labels (keys) to find the associated values.
- If you're tracking inventory in a warehouse, you might have items organized by bins or categories – a structured way to store and locate specific products.

Data structures in programming are the digital equivalents of these organizational systems. They provide a single variable that holds multiple values and give you defined ways to access, add, remove, or modify those values.

Why are data structures so important?

- **Managing Collections:** They allow you to handle large amounts of related data under a single name, rather than using countless individual variables.
- **Efficient Operations:** They provide built-in or standard ways to perform common tasks on the entire collection or specific items, such as:
  - Iterating through every item (e.g., using loops).
  - Finding a specific item.
  - Adding a new item.
  - Removing an existing item.
  - Sorting the items.

- **Organization and Readability:** They make your code clearer by grouping related data logically. Reading `for user in user_list:` is much more understandable than trying to loop through variables named `user1` through `user10`.
- **Scalability:** Your code becomes much easier to scale up. If your program needs to handle 1000 users instead of 10, you often don't need to change the logic for processing them if they are stored in a data structure; the same loop that works for 10 will work for 1000.

My personal programming journey involved a major leap forward once I started using data structures effectively. Simple programs that only dealt with one or two variables felt limiting. Learning about lists and dictionaries (which we'll cover in the rest of this chapter) opened up the possibility of writing programs that could manage groups of users, process multiple calculations, or store and retrieve complex sets of configuration settings. It's essential for moving beyond simple scripts to building real applications.

In this chapter, we'll focus on two fundamental data structures common in many programming languages: **Lists** (for ordered sequences) and **Dictionaries** (for key-value pairs). These will give you powerful new ways to organize the data your programs work with, building on the variables and data types you already understand.

That wraps up the conceptual need for data structures. You understand that they are essential for managing collections of data efficiently, performing operations on those collections, and making your code more organized and scalable.

8.2 Lists (or Arrays)

The most common data structure for storing an ordered sequence of items is a **List** (in Python) or an **Array** (in many other languages like JavaScript, Java, C++).

A List is like a container where you can store multiple values, and each value has a position (or index) starting from 0.

```
# data_structures.py

print("--- Lists ---")

# Creating a list
# Use square brackets [] to define a list
# Items are separated by commas
fruits = ["apple", "banana", "cherry", "date"]
numbers = [10, 20, 30, 40, 50]
```

```
mixed_list = ["hello", 123, True, 3.14] # Lists can hold items of different
data types

print("Fruits list:", fruits)
print("Numbers list:", numbers)
print("Mixed list:", mixed_list)
```

Save the file. Open your terminal, navigate to the directory, and run python data_structures.py.

```
--- Lists ---
Fruits list: ['apple', 'banana', 'cherry', 'date']
Numbers list: [10, 20, 30, 40, 50]
Mixed list: ['hello', 123, True, 3.14].
```

Step Explanation: We created lists by placing items inside square brackets [] and separating them with commas.

8.2.1 Creating Lists:

Alright, imagine you're tracking the high temperatures for the week. You *could* have variables like temp_monday = 75, temp_tuesday = 78, temp_wednesday = 72, and so on. But that's a pain! What if you had a year's worth of data? You'd have 365 separate variables!

This is where the idea of a **list** (or an array, as it's called in many other languages) becomes incredibly useful. A list is a data structure that allows you to store **multiple items in a single variable**. The items in a list are kept in a specific **order**.

Think of a list like items on a numbered or bulleted list you write down. The order matters (usually), and each item has a position.

In Python, creating a list is very straightforward. You use **square brackets []** to define the start and end of the list, and you separate the items inside the brackets with **commas ,**. You then assign this list to a variable using the assignment operator =.

Let's open our data_structures.py file again (or create it if you haven't already) and practice creating some lists.

```
# data_structures.py


print("--- Creating Lists ---")


# 1. Creating a list of strings
```

```python
# This list holds names
names = ["Alice", "Bob", "Charlie", "David"]
print("List of names:", names) # Output: List of names: ['Alice', 'Bob',
'Charlie', 'David']

# 2. Creating a list of numbers
# This list holds temperatures
temperatures = [75, 78, 72, 79, 81, 77, 76]
print("List of temperatures:", temperatures) # Output: List of temperatures:
[75, 78, 72, 79, 81, 77, 76]

# 3. Creating a list with items of different data types
# Lists are flexible! They can hold strings, numbers, booleans, or even other
lists/dictionaries
mixed_bag = ["hello", 123, True, 3.14, "world"]
print("Mixed list:", mixed_bag) # Output: Mixed list: ['hello', 123, True,
3.14, 'world']

# 4. Creating an empty list
# Sometimes you need a list to start empty and add items later
empty_list = []
print("An empty list:", empty_list) # Output: An empty list: []
```

Save the file. Open your terminal, navigate to the directory where you saved it, and run python data_structures.py.

Step Explanation:

1. names = ["Alice", "Bob", "Charlie", "David"]: We create a list containing four string values. The square brackets [] define the list, and the commas separate the items. The entire list is assigned to the variable names.
2. temperatures = [...]: Similar to the first, but this list holds integer numbers.
3. mixed_bag = [...]: This demonstrates that a single Python list can hold values of different data types simultaneously – a string, an integer, a boolean, a float, and another string. This flexibility is a characteristic of Python lists.
4. empty_list = []: To create a list with no items in it, you simply use empty square brackets []. This is common when you're going to collect items into a list later in your program (e.g., adding items based on user input or loop results).

My personal programs started feeling much more organized once I understood how to group related data into lists. Instead of managing item1, item2, item3, I could manage a single items list and then use loops (which we'll revisit in a later section on lists) to process each one. It immediately made my code cleaner and more scalable.

So, the core syntax for creating a list in Python is simple: [item1, item2, item3, ...]. The items can be variables or literal values, and they can be of any data type. The order in which you put them in is the order they will be stored.

8.2.2 Accessing Items by Index:

You can access individual items in a list using their **index**. The index is the item's position in the list, and **indexing starts at 0**.

```python
# data_structures.py - Add these examples


print("\n--- Accessing List Items by Index ---")


fruits = ["apple", "banana", "cherry", "date"]

# Access the first item (index 0)
first_fruit = fruits[0]
print("First fruit:", first_fruit) # Output: First fruit: apple


# Access the second item (index 1)
second_fruit = fruits[1]
print("Second fruit:", second_fruit) # Output: Second fruit: banana


# Access the last item (using negative index - Python specific feature)
last_fruit = fruits[-1]
print("Last fruit:", last_fruit) # Output: Last fruit: date


# Access an item using an invalid index will cause an error
# print(fruits[10]) # This would cause an IndexError


# Get the number of items in the list using the len() function
list_length = len(fruits)
print("Number of fruits:", list_length) # Output: Number of fruits: 4
```

Step Explanation: We use square brackets [] after the list variable name, putting the index number inside. len() is a built-in Python function that returns the number of items in a list (or other sequence).

8.2.3 Modifying Lists:

Lists are **mutable**, meaning you can change their contents after they are created – you can add items, remove items, or change items at specific indices.

```python
# data_structures.py - Add these examples

print("\n--- Modifying Lists ---")

numbers = [10, 20, 30, 40, 50]
print("Original numbers list:", numbers)

# Change an item at a specific index
numbers[2] = 35 # Change the item at index 2 (the number 30) to 35
print("After changing item at index 2:", numbers) # Output: After changing
item at index 2: [10, 20, 35, 40, 50]

# Add an item to the end of the list using the append() method
numbers.append(60)
print("After appending 60:", numbers) # Output: After appending 60: [10, 20,
35, 40, 50, 60]

# Remove an item by its value using the remove() method
numbers.remove(20) # Removes the first occurrence of the value 20
print("After removing 20:", numbers) # Output: After removing 20: [10, 35,
40, 50, 60]

# Remove an item by its index using the pop() method
removed_item = numbers.pop(0) # Removes the item at index 0 (the number 10)
and returns it
print("After popping item at index 0:", numbers) # Output: After popping item
at index 0: [35, 40, 50, 60]
print("Removed item:", removed_item) # Output: Removed item: 10

# You can also insert items at a specific index using insert()
# numbers.insert(1, 25) # Insert 25 at index 1
```

```
# print("After inserting 25 at index 1:", numbers) # Output: After inserting
25 at index 1: [35, 25, 40, 50, 60]
```

Step Explanation: Lists have built-in methods (functions that belong to the list object) like append(), remove(), pop(), and insert() that allow you to easily modify the list. We also directly assigned a new value to an item at a specific index (numbers[2] = 35).

8.2.4 Iterating Through Lists (Revisited: Loops)

Alright, you know how to create lists to hold collections of items, and you know how to access individual items by their index. That's great for getting one item at a time! But often, you need to *do something* with *every single item* in a list.

Imagine our list of temperatures for the week: [75, 78, 72, 79, 81, 77, 76]. What if you need to:

- Print each temperature with a label ("Monday: 75 degrees", "Tuesday: 78 degrees", etc.).
- Find the highest temperature.
- Calculate the average temperature.
- Convert each temperature from Fahrenheit to Celsius.

You *could* access each item by its index one by one:

```
# Inefficient way to process a list
temperatures = [75, 78, 72, 79, 81, 77, 76]
print("Temperature:", temperatures[0])
print("Temperature:", temperatures[1])
# ... imagine 5 more lines ...
print("Temperature:", temperatures[6])
```

Again, this is tedious and breaks if the list gets longer or shorter. This is exactly the kind of repetitive task that **loops** (from Chapter 6) are designed to handle, and **for loops** are particularly well-suited for working with lists.

Using a for Loop to Iterate Over List Items

As we briefly saw in Section 6.2, Python's for loop is designed to iterate directly over sequences like lists. It automatically goes through each item in the list, one by one, from beginning to end.

Let's revisit this in our data_structures.py file.

```
# data_structures.py - Add these examples
```

```python
print("\n--- Iterating Through Lists with FOR loop ---")

temperatures = [75, 78, 72, 79, 81, 77, 76]

# Use a for loop to process each item
for temp in temperatures:
    # Inside the loop, 'temp' holds the value of the current item
    print(f"Current temperature: {temp} degrees.")

print("Finished processing temperatures.")


print("\n--- FOR loop with Different List ---")

fruits = ["apple", "banana", "cherry"]

for fruit in fruits:
    # Process each fruit string
    print(f"I have a {fruit}.")

print("Finished processing fruits.")
```

Save and run the script.

```
--- Iterating Through Lists with FOR loop ---
Current temperature: 75 degrees.
Current temperature: 78 degrees.
Current temperature: 72 degrees.
Current temperature: 79 degrees.
Current temperature: 81 degrees.
Current temperature: 77 degrees.
Current temperature: 76 degrees.
Finished processing temperatures.

--- FOR loop with Different List ---
I have a apple.
I have a banana.
I have a cherry.
Finished processing fruits.
```

Step Explanation:

1. for temp in temperatures:: This line sets up the loop. It tells Python to iterate over the temperatures list. In the first iteration, the variable temp is automatically assigned the value of the first item in the list (75).
2. The code block indented below the for loop (print(f"Current temperature: {temp} degrees.")) is executed. Inside this block, temp currently holds 75.
3. After the block finishes, the loop goes to the next item in the temperatures list (78). In the second iteration, temp is assigned 78, and the block executes again.
4. This process continues until temp has been assigned and processed for the very last item in the list (76).
5. Once all items have been processed, the loop finishes, and the program continues after the indented block.
6. The second for loop demonstrates the same concept with a list of strings. The variable fruit takes on the value of each string in the fruits list in turn.

Commentary: This pattern (for item in list_name:) is incredibly common and powerful. It automatically handles knowing how many items are in the list and accessing each one in order. You don't need manual counters or index checks for basic iteration. The variable name you choose (temp, fruit, item, number) can be anything descriptive that represents a single element from the list.

Combining Iteration with Other Concepts

The real power comes when you combine iterating through lists with other concepts:

- **Iteration + Conditionals:** Process items differently based on their value or properties.
- **Iteration + Functions:** Call a function for each item or use a loop inside a function.
- **Iteration + Operators:** Perform calculations or comparisons on each item.

```python
# data_structures.py - Add these examples

print("\n--- Iteration with Conditionals (Finding High Temps) ---")

temperatures = [75, 78, 72, 79, 81, 77, 76]
high_temp_threshold = 78

print(f"Temperatures above {high_temp_threshold} degrees:")
for temp in temperatures:
    # Use an IF statement inside the loop
    if temp > high_temp_threshold:
        print(temp) # Print only the temperatures above the threshold
```

```python
print("\n--- Iteration with Calculation (Calculating Average) ---")

temperatures = [75, 78, 72, 79, 81, 77, 76]
total_temp = 0 # Initialize a variable outside the loop to accumulate the sum

for temp in temperatures:
    total_temp += temp # Add the current temperature to the total in each
iteration

average_temp = total_temp / len(temperatures) # Divide total by the number of
items

print(f"Total temperature sum: {total_temp}")
print(f"Average temperature: {average_temp}")

print("\n--- Iteration with Index (If you need position) ---")

# Sometimes you need both the item AND its index (position).
# You can use the enumerate() function for this.
temperatures = [75, 78, 72, 79, 81, 77, 76]
days = ["Mon", "Tue", "Wed", "Thu", "Fri", "Sat", "Sun"]

for index, temp in enumerate(temperatures):
    # enumerate() yields pairs: (index, item)
    day_label = days[index] # Use the index to get the day label from the
'days' list
    print(f"{day_label}: {temp} degrees")
```

Save and run.

Step Explanation:

1. **Iteration with Conditionals:** The if temp > high_temp_threshold: statement is inside the loop. It's checked for *each* temp as the loop iterates. The print(temp) only runs for those temperatures that satisfy the condition.
2. **Iteration with Calculation:** We initialize total_temp to 0 *before* the loop. Inside the loop, total_temp += temp adds the value of the current temp to total_temp in each iteration, accumulating the sum. After the loop, we use the len() function to get the total count of items and calculate the average.

3. **Iteration with Index:** enumerate(temperatures) is a Python function that's useful when you need both the index and the item while looping. It yields tuples (index, item) in each iteration. We unpack this tuple into two variables index, temp in the for statement. We then use the index variable to access the corresponding day name from the days list.

Using a for loop to iterate through lists is one of the most common and fundamental patterns in Python programming. It allows you to process collections of data efficiently and combine this iteration with your other programming tools like conditionals and calculations.

My programs became significantly more powerful once I could reliably iterate through lists and process each item. Whether it was displaying data from a file, processing user inputs stored in a list, or performing calculations on batches of numbers, loops + lists became a core part of my problem-solving approach.

You've revisited and solidified a crucial concept: **iterating through lists** using **for loops**. You understand how the for loop automatically processes each item in the list and how to combine this iteration with **conditionals** and **calculations** to perform complex operations on collections of data. You also saw how enumerate() is useful when you need access to the item's **index** during iteration.

This ability to process data structures efficiently using loops is essential for building useful programs. With lists and dictionaries to organize data, and loops to process them, you can now manage and work with collections of information effectively. Next, we'll look at Chapter 9 again, focusing on getting input and showing output, which are essential for interactive programs.

8.3 Introduction to Key-Value Pairs (Dictionaries or Objects)

Another fundamental data structure is used to store data as **key-value pairs**. This structure is called a **Dictionary** in Python, or an **Object** in JavaScript, or a Map in other languages.

Think of a physical dictionary or a phone book: you look up a word or a name (the key) to find its definition or phone number (the value). In a key-value pair structure, you store values associated with unique keys. Keys are typically strings or numbers.

8.3.1 What They Are:

A dictionary/object is an unordered collection of data where each item is stored as a pair: a unique **key** and its associated **value**.

```
# data_structures.py - Add these examples


print("\n--- Dictionaries (Key-Value Pairs) ---")
```

```python
# Creating a dictionary in Python
# Use curly braces {} to define a dictionary
# Key-value pairs are separated by colons (:)
# Pairs are separated by commas
user_profile = {
    "username": "Alice",
    "age": 30,
    "is_active": True,
    "city": "New York"
}

product = {
    "id": 101,
    "name": "Laptop",
    "price": 1200.00,
    "in_stock": 15,
    "tags": ["electronics", "computer", "laptop"] # Value can be a list or
another dictionary!
}

print("User profile:", user_profile)
print("Product details:", product)
```

Save and run.

```
--- Dictionaries (Key-Value Pairs) ---
User profile: {'username': 'Alice', 'age': 30, 'is_active': True, 'city':
'New York'}
Product details: {'id': 101, 'name': 'Laptop', 'price': 1200.0, 'in_stock':
15, 'tags': ['electronics', 'computer', 'laptop']}
```

Step Explanation: We created dictionaries using curly braces {}. Inside, we listed key-value pairs like "username": "Alice", separating the key and value with a colon :, and separating pairs with commas.

8.3.2 Accessing Values by Key:

You access the value associated with a key using square brackets [] with the key inside, or sometimes using dot notation (.) in certain languages like JavaScript (e.g., userProfile.age).

```python
# data_structures.py - Add these examples

print("\n--- Accessing Dictionary Values by Key ---")

user_profile = {
    "username": "Alice",
    "age": 30,
    "is_active": True,
    "city": "New York"
}

# Access values using the key
username = user_profile["username"]
print("Username:", username) # Output: Username: Alice

age = user_profile["age"]
print("Age:", age) # Output: Age: 30

# Accessing a key that doesn't exist will cause an error
# print(user_profile["email"]) # This would cause a KeyError

# Use the .get() method to safely access values (returns None if key not
found)
country = user_profile.get("country")
print("Country (using .get):", country) # Output: Country (using .get): None

# You can also provide a default value if the key is not found
email = user_profile.get("email", "N/A")
print("Email (using .get with default):", email) # Output: Email (using .get
with default): N/A



# You can modify values associated with a key
user_profile["age"] = 31 # Update the value for the key "age"
user_profile["city"] = "London"
print("Updated user profile:", user_profile) # Output: Updated user profile:
{'username': 'Alice', 'age': 31, 'is_active': True, 'city': 'London'}

# You can add new key-value pairs
```

```
user_profile["country"] = "USA"
print("User profile after adding country:", user_profile) # Output: User
profile after adding country: {'username': 'Alice', 'age': 31, 'is_active':
True, 'city': 'London', 'country': 'USA'}

# You can remove key-value pairs using del
del user_profile["city"]
print("User profile after deleting city:", user_profile) # Output: User
profile after deleting city: {'username': 'Alice', 'age': 31, 'is_active':
True, 'country': 'USA'}
```

Step Explanation: We used dictionary_variable[key] to get the value associated with a key. We also saw that this notation can be used to update existing values or add new key-value pairs. The del keyword removes a pair. The .get() method is a safer way to access values as it doesn't cause an error if the key doesn't exist.

8.4 Choosing the Right Structure

Deciding whether to use a List or a Dictionary (or other data structures you'll learn later) depends on how you need to organize and access your data:

- Use a **List** when:
    - You need an ordered sequence of items.
    - The position of items matters.
    - You want to access items by their index (position).
    - You need to iterate over *all* items in the collection.
- Use a **Dictionary** when:
    - You need to associate values with unique keys (names or identifiers).
    - The order of items doesn't inherently matter (though Python 3.7+ maintains insertion order).
    - You want to access items quickly by their key.

For instance, a list of student names might go in a List ["Alice", "Bob", "Charlie"]. But the details *about* a single student would likely go in a Dictionary {"name": "Alice", "student_id": "S123", "grade": "A"}. A list of *students* could be a List where each item in the list is a Dictionary representing a student: [{"name": "Alice", ...}, {"name": "Bob", ...}].

My advice here is to read the problem description and think about how you would organize that information in the real world. Is it a numbered list? Is it a lookup table? That intuition often guides you towards the right data structure.

You've taken another significant step by learning how to organize **collections** of data using **Lists** (ordered sequences accessed by index) and **Dictionaries** (unordered collections of key-value pairs accessed by key). You know how to create, access, modify, and iterate over these structures.

These data structures are essential for managing real-world data in your programs. They are the containers that hold the information your programs process. In the next chapter, we'll combine the concepts we've learned (variables, operators, control flow, functions, and data structures) to build simple, interactive programs that take input from the user and show them output.

Chapter 9
Getting Input and Showing Output

Alright! You're assembling some powerful programming tools. You can crunch numbers, evaluate conditions, and repeat tasks. Now, let's make your programs interactive. Most software isn't just a one-way street; it needs to communicate with the user or other systems – showing them information (output) and receiving information from them (input).

We've already done a fair bit of showing output using the print() function. Let's quickly revisit that, and then we'll focus on the other side of the conversation: getting input.

9.1 Review: Showing Output (Printing)

Alright, we've used it many times throughout the book already, but let's formally review the essential way your simple programs communicate with the outside world: showing output. In the context of the command-line scripts we've been writing, this primarily means displaying text in the terminal or console where you run your code.

The main tool for this in Python is the built-in **print()** function.

The print() function takes whatever you give it inside the parentheses () and displays its string representation in the standard output stream (which is usually your terminal). By default, after printing, it moves the cursor to the next line.

Think of it like your program talking directly to you through the console window. It's saying, "Hey, here's some information!"

Let's quickly confirm how it works with different types of data. We'll use our input_output_review.py file again.

```
# input_output_review.py


print("--- Showing Output Review ---")


# 1. Printing String Literals
# Displaying plain text messages enclosed in quotes
print("Hello from your program!")
print("Calculation Complete.")


# 2. Printing the Value of Variables
# Displaying the current value stored in a variable
my_message = "This is the value of a string variable."
```

```
print(my_message)

number_of_items = 5
print(number_of_items) # Prints the number 5 (converted to its string
representation)

is_available = True
print(is_available) # Prints the boolean True (converted to string "True")

pi_value = 3.14159
print(pi_value) # Prints the float (converted to string "3.14159")

# 3. Printing Multiple Items (Literals and Variables)
# Separate items with commas inside the print() function
print("The message is:", my_message, "Number of items:", number_of_items) #
Output: The message is: This is the value of a string variable. Number of
items: 5

# 4. Printing the Result of an Expression
# Evaluate an expression and print the result directly
print("10 + 20 is:", 10 + 20) # Output: 10 + 20 is: 30
print("Is 5 > 3?", 5 > 3) # Output: Is 5 > 3? True

# 5. Printing formatted output (using f-strings - introduced briefly in
Chapter 7)
# f-strings (formatted string literals) are a clean way to embed variable
values directly into strings
name = "Bob"
age = 25
print(f"User: {name}, Age: {age}") # Output: User: Bob, Age: 25
```

Save this code and run it from your terminal (python input_output_review.py). You'll see each print statement result in a line of output in your console.

Step Explanation:

1. When you put text in quotes inside print(), it prints that exact text.
2. When you put a variable name inside print(), it prints the *value* currently stored in that variable. Python automatically converts the value to its string representation before displaying it.

3. You can pass multiple arguments to print() separated by commas. By default, print() puts a space between each item it prints.
4. You can perform calculations or evaluations (like comparisons) directly inside print(), and it will display the final result.
5. Using **f-strings** (formatted string literals, starting the string with f before the opening quote) is a very convenient and readable way to include the values of variables directly within a string by putting the variable name in curly braces {}.

Commentary: print() is your window into your program's execution. When I'm debugging (Chapter 11), print() statements are my absolute best friends! I'll sprinkle them throughout my code to see what values variables hold at different points, which conditions are being met, or which lines of code are actually being executed. It's the simplest way to get feedback from your running program.

While this book focuses on console applications where print() is the main output method, remember that "showing output" in other programming domains involves different techniques:

- In **web development**, output is usually sending back HTML, CSS, and data (like JSON) to the user's browser, which the browser then renders visually.
- In **mobile app development**, output is updating the graphical user interface (GUI) on the phone's screen – displaying text labels, images, updating lists, etc.
- In **desktop software**, output is updating windows, menus, text areas, and other GUI elements.

Regardless of the specific method or interface, the core concept of the program communicating information back to the user remains the same. For our purposes in learning fundamentals with console scripts, print() is the key function.

This confirms your understanding of how to make your program "talk" to the user. This half of the conversation is crucial for debugging, displaying results, and prompting the user for input, which is the other half we'll dive into next.

9.2 Getting Input from the User

Now for the flip side! How does the program get information *from* the user?

Imagine a login screen asking for your username. The program needs to pause, wait for you to type something and press Enter, and then take the characters you typed and store them so it can check if they are correct.

In Python, the built-in function for getting text input from the user in the console is **input()**.

When your program reaches an input() call, it will:

1. Optionally display a message to the user (a **prompt**).
2. Pause execution.
3. Wait for the user to type text and press the Enter key.
4. Take the text the user typed.
5. Resume execution, and the value of the input() call will be the text the user typed.

Let's try a simple example in our input_output.py file.

```
# input_output.py - Add this after the print examples

print("\n--- Getting Input ---")


# Get input from the user
user_name = input("Please enter your name: ") # Display a prompt and wait for
input


# Now the program continues after the user presses Enter
print(f"Hello, {user_name}! Nice to meet you.")


print("Input example finished.")
```

Save and run the script.

```
--- Showing Output ---
Hello from your program!
The number of items is: 5
Calculation result: 30
True


--- Getting Input ---
Please enter your name:
```
Step Explanation:
1. The program prints the header "--- Getting Input ---".
2. It reaches the line user_name = input("Please enter your name: ").
3. It prints the prompt string "Please enter your name: " to the console.
4. It pauses and waits. A cursor will blink, indicating the program is waiting for your input.
5. Type your name (e.g., "Alice") and press Enter.
6. The input() function captures the text you typed ("Alice").
7. The = assignment operator stores that text in the user_name variable.

8. The program resumes execution and prints the next line, using the value now stored in user_name.

This is your program having its first conversation!

9.2.1 Handling Different Input Types

This is a really important point, and a common place where beginners encounter issues:

- **The input() function *always* returns the user's input as a string.**

Even if the user types numbers, like "30", input() gives you the string "30", not the number 30.

Why is this important? Because you can do arithmetic operations on numbers (like +), but the + operator performs concatenation on strings (joining them together).

Let's see this.

```
# input_output.py - Add this after the previous example

print("\n--- Input Data Type ---")

# Get a number from the user
num_str = input("Enter a number: ")
print("You entered:", num_str)
print("Type of input:", type(num_str)) # It's a string!

# What happens if we try to do math directly?
# This will cause a TypeError if you enter numbers, because you can't add a
string to 10 directly
# print("Adding 10 to your number:", num_str + 10) # ERROR!
# Or, if you entered "5", it would try "5" + 10 -> TypeError
# If you entered "5" and tried "5" + "10", it would concatenate: "510"
```

Save and run. Enter a number like 5. You'll see the type is str. If you uncomment the error line and run again, entering 5, you'll get a TypeError because you can't add a string and an integer.

Type Casting (Converting Data Types)

To perform mathematical operations on numbers received from input(), you must convert the input string into a numeric data type (like integer or float). This process is called **type casting** or **type conversion**.

Python provides functions for type casting:

- **int(value)**: Tries to convert value into an integer.
- **float(value)**: Tries to convert value into a floating-point number.
- **str(value)**: Tries to convert value into a string.
- **bool(value)**: Tries to convert value into a boolean.

```python
# input_output.py - Add this after the previous example

print("\n--- Type Casting Input ---")

# Get a number as a string
num_str = input("Enter a number to add 10 to: ")

# Convert the string to an integer using int()
# IMPORTANT: If the user types something that cannot be converted to an integer
# (like "hello" or "3.14"), this line will cause a ValueError!
try: # Use a try-except block to handle potential errors (more on this in Chapter 11)
    num_int = int(num_str) # Convert the string to an integer

    # Now we can do math with the integer
    result = num_int + 10
    print("Adding 10 to your number:", result) # Output: Adding 10 to your number: 15 (if user entered 5)
    print("Type after casting:", type(num_int)) # Output: Type after casting: <class 'int'>

except ValueError:
    print("Invalid input. Please enter a whole number.")


print("\n--- Casting to Float ---")

# Get a decimal number
decimal_str = input("Enter a decimal number: ")

try:
    decimal_float = float(decimal_str) # Convert the string to a float
```

```
    print("Your number as float:", decimal_float)
    print("Type after casting:", type(decimal_float))

except ValueError:
    print("Invalid input. Please enter a number with or without decimals.")
```

Save and run. Try entering a whole number first. Then run it again and try entering a decimal number. Then run it a third time and try entering text like "hello" to see the error message from the try-except block.

Step Explanation:

1. We get the input as a string using input().
2. We wrap the int() conversion in a try-except ValueError block. This tells Python to try the code in the first indented block. If a ValueError occurs during the int() conversion (because the string wasn't a valid integer), the program doesn't crash; instead, it jumps to the except ValueError: block and executes the code there.
3. Inside the try block, int(num_str) attempts the conversion. If successful, the integer value is stored in num_int.
4. We can now safely perform arithmetic (num_int + 10) because num_int is an integer.
5. The second example shows casting to a float using float(), also within a try-except block to handle invalid input.

This is a fundamental pattern when dealing with user input: **get input as a string, then explicitly cast it to the desired data type (like int or float) using type casting functions, handling potential errors (like ValueError) if the input isn't in the expected format.**

9.3 Combining Input, Processing, and Output

Now that you know how to get input, you can combine it with everything else you've learned to build simple interactive programs.

```
# input_output.py - Add this after the type casting examples

print("\n--- Interactive Program Example (Age Check) ---")

try:
    # 1. Get input from the user (as a string)
    age_str = input("Please enter your age: ")

    # 2. Convert input to the correct data type (integer)
```

```python
    user_age = int(age_str)

    # 3. Process the data (using comparison operators and conditional
statements)
    if user_age >= 18:
        # 4. Show output based on processing
        print("You are old enough to vote!")
    else:
        print("You are not old enough to vote yet.")

except ValueError:
    # Handle invalid input during casting
    print("That wasn't a valid number for age. Please enter a whole number.")

print("Age check program finished.")


print("\n--- Interactive Program Example 2 (Simple Calculator) ---")

try:
    # Get two numbers and an operation
    num_str1 = input("Enter first number: ")
    num_str2 = input("Enter second number: ")
    operation = input("Enter operation (+, -, *, /): ")

    # Convert numbers to float (allows for decimals)
    num1 = float(num_str1)
    num2 = float(num_str2)

    # Perform the operation based on input (using conditional statements)
    if operation == "+":
        result = num1 + num2
        print(f"Result: {result}")
    elif operation == "-":
        result = num1 - num2
        print(f"Result: {result}")
    elif operation == "*":
        result = num1 * num2
        print(f"Result: {result}")
```

```
    elif operation == "/":
        if num2 != 0: # Prevent division by zero!
            result = num1 / num2
            print(f"Result: {result}")
        else:
            print("Error: Cannot divide by zero.")
    else:
        print("Invalid operation.")


except ValueError:
    print("Invalid input. Please enter valid numbers.")
```

Save and run. Try the age check (enter numbers, enter text). Then try the simple calculator (enter numbers and operations, try dividing by zero, try invalid input).

Step Explanation: These examples bring together almost everything we've learned:

- **Input:** Getting data using input().
- **Variables & Types:** Storing input in variables, understanding it's a string, using type casting (int(), float()) to convert it.
- **Error Handling:** Using try-except to catch errors during type casting.
- **Operators:** Using comparison (>=, !=) and arithmetic (+, -, *, /) operators.
- **Control Flow:** Making decisions using if-else and if-elif-else based on the input and calculations.
- **Output:** Showing the result or messages using print().

This process of Input -> Process -> Output is a fundamental pattern in many programs. You get data, you do something with it, and you show the result.

My personal programs became much more engaging and useful once I learned how to get input. I could stop just writing scripts that did the same thing every time and start writing programs that felt like conversations, reacting differently based on what I (or a user) typed in.

Mini-Project Idea Tease: The ability to get user input and show output is essential for interactive software. You'll use these skills directly when we build our mini-project in the next chapter! Projects like guessing games or simple text adventures rely heavily on this back-and-forth interaction with the user.

You've reached another critical milestone! You now know how to make your programs interactive by getting input from the user using input() and, crucially, how to handle that input by understanding that it's initially a string and using type casting (int(), float()) to convert it for calculations, while also handling potential errors. You've seen how combining input, processing (with variables, operators, control flow), and output allows you to build meaningful programs.

This ability to communicate with the user unlocks a whole new level of software complexity and usefulness. In the next chapter, we'll take all the fundamental concepts we've learned – variables, operators, control flow, functions, data structures, input, and output – and apply them together to build your first complete piece of software as a mini-project! Get ready to build!

Chapter 10
Building Your First Piece of Software (Mini-Project)

Alright! You've climbed the conceptual mountain, learning the fundamental building blocks of programming. You know the grammar and basic vocabulary. Now, it's time to write your first short story – your first piece of actual software!

This chapter is dedicated to applying everything you've learned by building a mini-project. This is where you'll see how variables, loops, decisions, functions, and input/output work together in a small, functional program.

Choosing a project that's just the right size is important. It should be big enough to require combining several concepts, but small enough to be achievable without getting overwhelmed. Good beginner mini-projects often involve interaction, decision-making, and perhaps some repetition.

Some classic choices include:

- **Simple Calculator:** Takes two numbers and an operation, then prints the result. (We did a basic version in the last chapter, but could expand it).
- **Guessing Game:** The computer picks a random number, and the user tries to guess it, getting hints (higher/lower) until they get it right.
- **Basic Text Adventure:** Present the user with choices in a simple story ("You are in a room. There is a door to the north and a key on the table. What do you do?"), and the program responds based on their text input.

Let's build a **Guessing Game**. It's interactive, requires decision-making (if/else for hints and winning), repetition (while loop to keep guessing), variables to store the secret number and guess, and input/output to talk to the user.

My personal experience with mini-projects was transformative. It was one thing to understand loops or functions in isolation, but actually *using* them together to make something that *did* something felt completely different. There were moments of frustration when the logic didn't work as planned, but the satisfaction when the little program finally ran correctly was immense. This is where the concepts start to click and feel real.

10.1 Planning Your Project (The Guessing Game)

Alright, you're ready to build your first piece of software. This is where all the fundamental concepts you've learned start coming together in a tangible way. But just like you wouldn't start building a house by randomly stacking bricks, you don't start programming a project by randomly typing code. The first step is always **planning**.

Planning your project, even a small one like our Guessing Game, involves defining what the program should do and outlining the steps needed to achieve that. This helps you clarify your thoughts, anticipate potential issues, and break down the task into smaller, manageable pieces that you know how to code based on the fundamentals you've learned.

When I first started, I would often skip the planning phase, eager to just jump into writing code. This almost always led to getting stuck quickly, realizing I hadn't thought through a necessary step, or having to rewrite large parts of the code. Taking even just 10-15 minutes to plan out a small project saves immense time and frustration later on. It's like looking at a map before starting a journey.

Choosing the Right Project Size:

For your first project applying all the fundamentals, it's important to choose something that is:

- **Small enough** to complete without getting overwhelmed.
- **Large enough** to require using a combination of concepts (variables, decisions, loops, input/output).
- **Interactive** (console-based is perfect for now) so you can see input and output in action.

Classic beginner projects fit this well:

- A simple calculator (handles different operations).
- A text-based game (like Guessing Game, or Rock Paper Scissors).
- A basic quiz or survey.
- A unit converter.

We've chosen the **Number Guessing Game** for this chapter because it neatly requires input/output, variables, loops, and decision-making – hitting many of the key fundamentals we've covered.

Defining the Project Requirements:

The first part of planning is clearly stating what the program should do. For our Number Guessing Game, let's define the requirements:

1. The program needs to **select a random whole number** for the user to guess. We need to decide on the **range** for this number (e.g., between 1 and 20).
2. The program needs to **prompt the user** to enter their guess.
3. The program needs to **read** the user's guess.
4. The program needs to **check if the guess is correct**.
5. If the guess is incorrect, the program needs to **provide a hint**: tell the user if their guess was **too high** or **too low**.
6. The program should **allow the user to guess multiple times** until they get it right.

7. We should probably limit the user to a **maximum number of guesses** to prevent the game from potentially going on forever.
8. If the user guesses correctly, the program should **congratulate them** and tell them **how many guesses it took**.
9. If the user runs out of guesses before getting it right, the program should **tell them they lost** and reveal the secret number.
10. The program should **handle invalid input** if the user types something that isn't a number.

These requirements describe the desired behavior of our software.

Outlining the Program Flow:

Based on the requirements, we can outline the sequence of steps the program needs to follow. This is often called creating a **program flow** or a simple **algorithm**. You can write this out in plain English or even draw a simple diagram.

For the Guessing Game, a possible flow might look like this:

1. **Start the game:** Greet the user, explain the rules.
2. **Setup:**
   - Pick the random secret number.
   - Set the number of guesses made so far to zero.
   - Set the maximum number of guesses allowed.
   - Keep track of whether the user has guessed correctly (initially no).
3. **Repeat the following steps** (this is our loop!):
   - *Check if the user still has guesses left.* If not, exit the loop.
   - *If guesses are left:*
     - Tell the user how many guesses they have remaining.
     - Ask the user to enter their guess (Input).
     - Read the user's input.
     - *Attempt to convert the input into a number.*
     - *If conversion fails (invalid input):* Tell the user it's invalid and go back to the start of the repeat block (ask for input again).
     - *If conversion succeeds:*
       - Increment the guess counter.
       - *Compare the user's guess to the secret number.*
       - *If the guess is too high:* Tell the user "Too high!"
       - *If the guess is too low:* Tell the user "Too low!"
       - *If the guess is correct:* Tell the program the user guessed correctly and exit the repeat block immediately.

4. **Game Over:**
   - ○ *Check if the user guessed correctly* (this is *why* the repeat block stopped).
   - ○ *If they guessed correctly:* Print a winning message, including the number of guesses.
   - ○ *If they did NOT guess correctly (they ran out of guesses):* Print a losing message, revealing the secret number.
5. **End the program.**

This detailed flow includes the major steps, indicates where decisions need to be made, where repetition is required, and where input/output happens. It directly uses the fundamental programming concepts we've learned (Input/Output, Variables, Loops, Decisions, Error Handling).

My personal planning often starts with a messy handwritten list like this, drawing arrows or indentation to show loops and decisions. The goal isn't a perfect formal document, but a clear roadmap for *me* to follow when I start writing the code. It helps ensure I don't forget key steps like initializing counters or handling invalid input.

Planning doesn't have to take hours for a mini-project, but spending even 15-20 minutes thinking through the requirements and outlining the steps will make the coding process much smoother and less prone to getting stuck on fundamental logic issues. It ensures you have a clear picture of what you're building before you start typing.

You've now learned the crucial first step in building any software: **planning**. You understand the importance of defining **requirements** for your project and outlining the logical **program flow** (or algorithm) before writing code. You've applied this process to plan out a Number Guessing Game, breaking it down into manageable steps involving initialization, a main loop, processing guesses, and handling the game over condition.

This planning phase is essential for translating your ideas into a blueprint that can be coded. In the next section (10.2), we'll start translating this plan into actual Python code, implementing the features step-by-step.

10.2 Breaking Down the Problem

Alright, you have the blueprint for your Guessing Game from the planning phase. It lists the main stages: Initialization, the Game Loop, Handling Each Guess, and Game Over. That's a great start, but each of those stages still contains multiple individual tasks that need to be translated into specific lines of code.

Breaking down a problem means taking a large task and dividing it into smaller, simpler sub-tasks that you know how to implement using the programming fundamentals you've learned (variables, operators, input/output, control flow, functions, data structures). You keep breaking down tasks until they are small enough to translate directly into a few lines of code.

Think about making that cake recipe again. The overall goal is "Bake a Chocolate Cake". You break it down into main steps: "Prepare Ingredients", "Mix Batter", "Bake Cake", "Make Frosting", "Assemble and Decorate". But "Mix Batter" is still too big for a single instruction. You break *that* down: "Cream butter and sugar", "Beat in eggs", "Combine dry ingredients", "Add dry and wet ingredients alternately", etc. You continue until each step is a single, actionable instruction like "Add 1 cup of flour".

For programming, the "actionable instructions" are the fundamental operations we've learned:

- Assign a value to a variable.
- Perform an arithmetic calculation.
- Get input from the user.
- Compare two values.
- Loop a certain number of times.
- Call a specific function.

Let's revisit our Guessing Game plan and break down the key stages into these smaller coding-level steps.

Breaking Down the Guessing Game Plan:

Here's our high-level plan again:

1. Initialization
2. Main Game Loop (while guessing is needed)
3. Inside the Loop (Handle Each Guess)
4. After the Loop (Game Over)

Now, let's break down each of these points into concrete programming tasks.

1. Initialization:

- *Choose a random secret number:* How do we do this?
    - Need a way to generate randomness. (We'll need to use a tool/function from the language's libraries for this).
    - Need to specify the range (1 to 20).
    - Need to store the result in a variable.
    - *Task:* Use a random number function (like `random.randint(1, 20)` in Python) and assign its result to a variable `secret_number`.
- *Initialize a counter for the number of guesses:*
    - Need a variable to count guesses.

- o Need to start counting from zero or one.
- o *Task:* Create a variable `guess_count` and assign it the initial value `0`.
- *Set the maximum number of guesses allowed:*
  - o Need a variable to store the limit.
  - o Decide the limit (e.g., 6).
  - o *Task:* Create a variable `max_guesses` and assign it the value `6`.
- *Keep track of whether the user has guessed correctly:*
  - o Need a variable (probably boolean) to indicate this.
  - o Initially, the user hasn't guessed correctly.
  - o *Task:* Create a variable `guessed_correctly` and assign it the initial value `False`. (Or, as we did in the Chapter 10 full code example, use the `user_guess` variable and initialize it to `None` or a value outside the range, checking `user_guess == secret_number` in the loop condition).

2. Main Game Loop:

- *Repeat the following steps...* We need a loop that continues as long as the user hasn't won *and* they still have guesses left.
  - o Need a `while` loop because the number of iterations isn't fixed.
  - o Need a condition for the `while` loop: it continues if the user has *not* guessed correctly AND the current guess count is less than the maximum allowed.
  - o *Task:* Write `while not guessed_correctly and guess_count < max_guesses:`. (Or `while user_guess != secret_number and guess_count < max_guesses:` if using the `user_guess` variable).

3. Inside the Loop (Handle Each Guess):

- *Check if the user still has guesses left.* If not, exit loop. (This is handled by the `while` loop condition itself).
- *If guesses are left:*
  - o *Tell the user how many guesses they have remaining:*
    - ▪ Need to calculate remaining guesses (`max_guesses - guess_count`).
    - ▪ Need to print a message including this calculation and the current guess number.
    - ▪ *Task:* Use `print(f"You have {max_guesses - guess_count} guesses left. Guess #{guess_count + 1}: ")`.
  - o *Ask the user to enter their guess (Input):*
    - ▪ Need to get input from the user.
    - ▪ *Task:* Use `input(...)` and store the result in a string variable `guess_str`.
  - o *Attempt to convert the input into a number:*

- Need to convert the string `guess_str` to an integer.
- Need to handle the possibility of invalid input (non-numbers) gracefully.
- *Task:* Use a `try...except ValueError` block around `int(guess_str)`.
  - o *If conversion fails:*
    - Tell the user about the invalid input.
    - Skip the rest of this guess's logic and go to the next loop iteration.
    - *Task:* Inside the `except` block, `print("Invalid input...")` and `continue`.
  - o *If conversion succeeds:*
    - Store the converted number in a variable (e.g., `user_guess`).
    - Increment the guess counter.
    - *Task:* `user_guess = int(guess_str)` (inside `try`), `guess_count += 1`.
    - *Compare the user's guess to the secret number:*
      - Need to check if `user_guess` is less than, greater than, or equal to `secret_number`.
      - Need `if/elif/else`.
      - *If the guess is too high:* Tell the user.
      - *If the guess is too low:* Tell the user.
      - *If the guess is correct:* Change the "guessed correctly" variable to `True`. (Or the loop condition `user_guess != secret_number` will become false).
    - *Task:* `if user_guess < secret_number: print("Too low!")`, `elif user_guess > secret_number: print("Too high!")`. If using the `guessed_correctly` flag: `else: guessed_correctly = True`.

4. After the Loop (Game Over):

- *Check why the loop finished:* Did `guessed_correctly` become `True` or did `guess_count` reach `max_guesses`?
  - o Need an `if/else` after the loop.
  - o *Task:* `if guessed_correctly: ...` (Or `if user_guess == secret_number: ...`)
- *If they guessed correctly:* Print a winning message, including the secret number and `guess_count`.
  - o *Task:* `print(f"Congratulations! ... took you {guess_count} guesses.")`.
- *If they did NOT guess correctly (they ran out of guesses):* Print a losing message, revealing the secret number.

○ *Task:* `else: print(f"Sorry, you ran out of guesses! ... number was {secret_number}.")`.

My personal experience breaking down problems is that it often involves figuring out how to use boolean flags (like `guessed_correctly`) or checks based on the loop variables (like `guess_count` or `user_guess`) to control the flow both *during* the loop and to understand the outcome *after* the loop finishes. Also, identifying where input conversion and validation need to happen and adding `try-except` and `continue` (or `break`) statements to handle bad input gracefully is crucial.

This detailed breakdown is much easier to translate into code than the high-level plan. Each bullet point here represents a specific action you can now implement using the functions, operators, control flow, and input/output methods you've learned.

Connecting Breakdown to Code:

- "Choose a random number": Need `import random` and `random.randint(...)`.
- "Store in a variable": Need `=`.
- "Ask the user to enter their guess": Need `print()` for the prompt, `input()` to get the string.
- "Convert the input string to a number": Need `int(...)` or `float(...)`.
- "Handle invalid input": Need `try...except ValueError`.
- "Skip the rest of this guess": Need `continue`.
- "Check if the guess is correct": Need `if user_guess == secret_number:`.
- "Provide a hint (too high/low)": Need `elif user_guess > secret_number: print("Too high!")` and `else: print("Too low!")`.
- "Repeat the following steps": Need a `while` loop.
- "Keep asking until the user gets it right AND they haven't run out of guesses": Need the loop condition `while user_guess != secret_number and guess_count < max_guesses:`.
- "Increment the guess counter": Need `guess_count += 1`.
- "Check why the loop finished": Need `if user_guess == secret_number: ... else: ...` after the loop.
- "Print a winning/losing message": Need `print()`.

This is the process of mapping the problem's logic to specific programming constructs.

You've successfully tackled the critical step of **breaking down the problem**! You understand how to take the requirements and overall flow from the planning phase and divide them into smaller, concrete programming tasks that can be implemented using the fundamental concepts you've learned. You saw how to break down the Guessing Game into specific steps involving variables, input/output, type casting, error handling, comparisons, and control flow using `if`/`elif`/`else` and `while` loops.

10.3 Implementing Features Step-by-Step

Let's start coding! We'll build this program piece by piece. Open your code editor and create a new file, guessing_game.py.

```python
# guessing_game.py

# Your first mini-project: A number guessing game!

import random # We need the random module to generate a random number

print("Welcome to the Guessing Game!")
print("I'm thinking of a number between 1 and 20.")

# --- Step 1: Initialization ---

# Choose a random number between 1 and 20 (inclusive)
secret_number = random.randint(1, 20) # random.randint(a, b) includes both a
and b
# print(f"(DEBUG: The secret number is {secret_number})") # Uncomment for
debugging!

# Initialize the guess counter
guess_count = 0

# Set the maximum number of guesses allowed
max_guesses = 6

# Variable to store the user's guess (initialize as None or a value that
isn't the secret number)
# We need a way to know if the user has guessed correctly to control the loop
user_guess = None # Using None means the user hasn't guessed yet

# --- Step 2: Main Game Loop ---
# The loop continues as long as the user hasn't guessed correctly (user_guess
!= secret_number)
```

```python
    # AND they haven't exceeded the maximum number of guesses (guess_count <
max_guesses)
while user_guess != secret_number and guess_count < max_guesses:

    # --- Step 3: Inside the Loop (Each Guess) ---

    # Prompt the user and get their input
    guess_str = input(f"You have {max_guesses - guess_count} guesses left.
Enter your guess: ")

    # Convert the input string to an integer
    # Add basic error handling for non-integer input (like we discussed in
Chapter 9 and will formalize in Chapter 11)
    try:
        user_guess = int(guess_str) # Try to convert to integer

        # Add a check to ensure the guess is within the valid range (1-20)
        if user_guess < 1 or user_guess > 20:
            print("Please guess a number between 1 and 20.")
            # Don't increment guess_count for invalid input outside the
range, or if casting failed
            continue # Use 'continue' to skip the rest of this loop iteration
and ask again

    except ValueError:
        # If int() failed, handle the error
        print("Invalid input. Please enter a whole number.")
        # Don't increment guess_count for invalid input
        continue # Use 'continue' to skip the rest of this loop iteration

    # If we reached here, input was a valid integer within the range (1-20)
    # Increment the guess counter (we only count valid guesses)
    guess_count += 1

    # Compare the guess to the secret number (Decision)
    if user_guess < secret_number:
        print("Too low!")
    elif user_guess > secret_number:
        print("Too high!")
```

```
    # If user_guess == secret_number, the loop condition (user_guess !=
secret_number) becomes False, and the loop will exit naturally


# --- Step 4: After the Loop ---

# Check why the loop finished (Decision)
if user_guess == secret_number:
    # User guessed correctly
    print(f"\nCongratulations! You guessed the number {secret_number}
correctly!")
    print(f"It took you {guess_count} guesses.")
else:
    # User ran out of guesses
    print("\nSorry, you ran out of guesses!")
    print(f"The number I was thinking of was {secret_number}.")


print("\nGame Over.")
```

Save the file. Open your terminal, navigate to the directory, and run python guessing_game.py. Play the game! Try entering numbers, try entering text, try entering numbers outside the range. See how the program responds.

10.4 Combining Functions, Data Structures, and Control Flow

Even this relatively simple game uses many concepts:

- **Input/Output:** input() to get guesses, print() to show messages.
- **Variables:** secret_number, guess_count, max_guesses, user_guess, guess_str, result_message.
- **Data Types:** Integers, strings, booleans (user_guess != secret_number, guess_count < max_guesses, results of comparisons).
- **Operators:** Arithmetic (+, -), comparison (<, >), assignment (=, +=), logical (and, not - implicitly used in the while condition).
- **Control Flow (Loops):** A while loop to repeat the guessing process.
- **Control Flow (Decisions):** if/elif/else to compare the guess and determine the outcome after the loop. Nested if inside the try block to check the range.
- **Functions:** Using built-in functions like print(), input(), int(), float(), type(), len() (though not directly used here), random.randint().
- **Error Handling (Basic):** Using try-except ValueError to prevent the program from crashing if the user enters non-integer input.

- **Modules:** Importing the random module to use the randint() function.

We didn't explicitly define *our own* functions or use complex data structures like Lists of Dictionaries in this *specific* simple game, but we easily *could* have! For example, if we wanted to record every guess the user made, we could store them in a **List** and append() each guess to the list inside the loop. If we wanted different difficulty levels with different ranges and guess limits, we could use a **Dictionary** to store those settings (difficulty_settings = {"easy": {"range": 10, "guesses": 10}, ...}). If the game had different phases (setup, guessing, game over), we could create **Functions** for each phase (def setup_game():, def play_round():, def end_game():) and call them sequentially in the main program flow.

This shows how the concepts fit together. Data structures hold your organized information. Operators work on that data. Control flow decides *when* and *how many times* those operations happen. Functions group related operations into reusable blocks. Input and Output allow the program to interact with the outside world.

10.5 Testing Your Software (Basic Verification)

Alright, the code for your Number Guessing Game is written! You've assembled variables, loops, decisions, input, and output according to your plan. You've built your first piece of software!

Now comes a critical step that often gets overlooked by beginners eager to declare victory: **testing your software**. Testing means running your code and verifying that it behaves exactly as you intended under different circumstances.

Think about any product you use – a phone, a car, a website. They were all tested extensively before being released to make sure they work correctly and don't have bugs that cause problems. Your software needs the same care!

For a small, simple program like our guessing game run in the terminal, "testing" means **manual verification**. This isn't the formal, automated testing you'll learn about for larger projects (which uses code to test code!), but it's essential for confirming that your program's logic is correct.

My early days involved a lot of writing code, running it once with some basic input, seeing that it didn't crash, and assuming it worked. Then I'd show it to someone else, and they'd try something slightly different, and a bug would immediately appear! This quickly taught me that testing isn't just running the program; it's running it *strategically* to try and find where it might break or misbehave.

Why Test Your Software?
- **Find Bugs:** The most obvious reason – uncover errors that prevent your program from running or producing the correct results.
- **Verify Logic:** Confirm that the decisions and loops in your code are working according to your intended plan.

- **Handle Edge Cases:** Test inputs or scenarios that are outside the most common or expected uses (e.g., entering zero, entering text, entering numbers on the boundary of a range).
- **Build Confidence:** Knowing you've tried various scenarios gives you confidence that your software is reliable.

Manual Verification Strategy for the Guessing Game:

For our `guessing_game.py` program, manual verification involves running the script multiple times and intentionally trying different inputs and scenarios to see how the program responds.

1. **Run the Script:** Open your terminal, navigate to where you saved `guessing_game.py`, and run `python guessing_game.py`.
2. **Test the "Happy Path":** Try playing the game normally and winning *within* the guess limit.
    - Enter a guess.
    - See if the hint (too high/low) is correct.
    - Adjust your next guess based on the hint.
    - Continue until you guess the secret number.
    - Verify the winning message is correct and shows the right number of guesses.
3. **Test Edge Cases for Winning:**
    - Try to guess the secret number on your *very first* guess. Does it work? Is the guess count correct (1)?
    - Try to guess the secret number on your *very last* allowed guess. Does it work? Is the guess count correct (e.games, 6)?
4. **Test the "Unhappy Path":** What happens if the user *doesn't* win?
    - Intentionally guess incorrectly multiple times until you run out of guesses.
    - Verify that the program correctly detects you ran out of guesses.
    - Verify that the losing message is displayed.
    - Verify that the losing message reveals the correct secret number.
5. **Test Input Validation:** How does the program handle bad input?
    - When prompted for a guess, enter text that is clearly not a number (e.g., "hello", "I don't know").
    - Verify that your `try-except ValueError` block catches this.
    - Verify that the program prints your "Invalid input. Please enter a whole number." message.
    - Verify that the program prompts you for a guess *again* and doesn't count the invalid input towards your guess limit.
    - When prompted for a guess, enter a number with a decimal (e.g., "10.5"). Does your `int()` conversion handle this? (It shouldn't cause a `ValueError` in this case,

as `int()` expects whole numbers only). Verify the error message is appropriate (or that it works if you had used `float()`).

- When prompted for a guess, enter a number outside the valid range (e.g., -5 or 100, if the range is 1-20). Verify that the code checks for this range and gives the correct message ("Please guess a number between 1 and 20."). Verify it doesn't count this invalid input towards the limit.

6. **Test Boundaries:** For the range check (1 to 20), specifically test the boundaries.
   - Guess `1`. Does it give a "Too low!" hint if the number is 1? (No, it should be correct). Does it give a "Too low!" hint if the number is 2? Yes.
   - Guess `20`. Does it give a "Too high!" hint if the number is 20? (No, it should be correct). Does it give a "Too high!" hint if the number is 19? Yes.

This systematic process of thinking about different inputs and scenarios, including the less obvious ones, is the core of testing. It moves beyond just confirming the basic functionality works to trying to find the points where the program might behave unexpectedly.

My strategy is usually to list out the different conditions and inputs I want to test based on the requirements and my understanding of the code's logic (especially around `if/else` statements, loop conditions, and input conversions). Then I run the program and try each scenario specifically.

Using Debugging Techniques During Testing:

If you encounter a bug during manual testing (the program crashes, gives the wrong output, or gets stuck), use the debugging techniques you learned in Chapter 11:

1. Read the error message/traceback carefully.
2. Go to the file and line number indicated.
3. Add `print()` statements before and after the problematic line to inspect the values of key variables and confirm the program's path.
4. Form a hypothesis about what's wrong and try to fix it.
5. Repeat the test scenario to see if the fix worked.

Testing and debugging go hand-in-hand. Testing reveals the presence of bugs; debugging helps you find their source so you can fix them.

You've completed the essential step of **testing your software** through **manual verification**! You understand why testing is crucial and how to apply a systematic approach to running your program with different inputs and scenarios, including happy paths, unhappy paths, edge cases, and invalid input. You also know how to use your debugging skills if testing reveals a bug.

10.6 Refactoring and Improving Your Code

After you get your program working, it's a great practice to **refactor** it. Refactoring means restructuring your code – making it cleaner, more readable, or more efficient – *without* changing what the program actually does.

For our guessing game, we could refactor it by:

- Moving the initial setup logic into a setup_game() function.
- Moving the logic for getting and validating a single guess into a get_valid_guess() function that returns the valid number or signals an error.
- Moving the game-over logic into an end_game() function.

This would make the main part of the script shorter and clearer, essentially looking like:

```python
# guessing_game_refactored.py (Conceptual)

import random

# Define functions here (setup_game, get_valid_guess, end_game)

# --- Main Program Flow ---
secret_number, guess_count, max_guesses = setup_game()

while guess_count < max_guesses:
    user_guess = get_valid_guess(max_guesses - guess_count) # Function gets input and handles errors

    if user_guess is not None: # If get_valid_guess returned a valid number
        guess_count += 1
        if user_guess < secret_number:
            print("Too low!")
        elif user_guess > secret_number:
            print("Too high!")
        else: # Guess is correct!
            break # Exit the loop early

end_game(user_guess, secret_number, guess_count)

print("\nGame Over.")
```

This refactored version is more organized. The main flow is easy to read, and the details of setup, getting input, and ending the game are hidden away inside their respective functions. This is a common practice as programs grow.

My personal experience with refactoring is that while it feels like extra work *after* the program is working, it makes adding *new* features or fixing bugs *later* much, much easier. It's an investment in the future maintainability of your code. Don't be afraid to rewrite parts of your code to make them cleaner once you understand the logic better.

You've just built your first complete piece of software by combining all the fundamental concepts you've learned in this book! You planned the logic, broke down the problem, implemented it step-by-step using variables, operators, control flow, functions, data structures, and input/output. You also got a taste of testing and refactoring.

This mini-project is a significant milestone. It shows you can think like a programmer and translate a problem into working code. You have now moved from understanding concepts in isolation to applying them in a complete program.

In the final chapter, we'll summarize everything you've learned and look at the vast and exciting directions you can take next in your programming journey. Get ready to explore the future!

Chapter 11
Dealing with Mistakes: Errors and Debugging

Alright, take a deep breath. If there's one universal truth in programming, it's this: your code will have errors. It's not a sign that you're bad at this; it's a completely normal and expected part of the process. Even experienced developers write code with bugs!

The difference between a frustrated beginner and a developing programmer isn't whether they make errors, but how they *deal* with them. Learning to see errors not as frustrating roadblocks, but as helpful clues in a detective story, is a key mindset shift.

This chapter is your guide to understanding those clues and becoming a code detective. The process of finding and fixing errors is called **debugging**.

My early days of coding were filled with moments of staring at error messages, convinced the computer was mocking me. Nothing seemed to make sense! It felt like hitting a brick wall. But over time, I learned to slow down, read the messages, and use simple techniques to figure out what was actually going wrong. Debugging is a skill, and like any skill, it improves with practice.

11.1 Understanding Different Types of Errors

Errors can happen at different stages of your program's life and for different reasons. We can generally categorize them into three main types:

11.1.1 Syntax Errors

Alright, let's talk about the first type of obstacle you'll face when your code doesn't run perfectly: **Syntax Errors**. These are like the grammar mistakes of programming. Every programming language has specific rules for how code must be written – where parentheses go, when to use colons, how to spell keywords, etc. If you break these rules, you've made a syntax error.

Think about telling someone to bake a cake using a recipe, but you write, "Mix the flour and sugar, then) add eggs." The person reading the instruction would stop at the unmatched parenthesis and say, "I don't understand this sentence structure." They can't even start mixing because the instruction itself is malformed.

Syntax errors are similar. They happen when the computer (specifically, the interpreter or compiler trying to read your code) encounters code that doesn't follow the expected structure of the programming language. It can't even understand *what* you're trying to tell it to do on that line because the command isn't formed correctly.

Why They Happen:

Syntax errors happen due to simple mistakes in typing or structuring your code:

- **Typos:** Misspelling a keyword (prnt instead of print).
- **Missing Punctuation:** Forgetting a colon : after an if statement or function definition.
- **Mismatched Delimiters:** Having an opening parenthesis (without a closing one), or an opening quote " without a closing one.
- **Incorrect Indentation:** In Python, incorrect indentation (using spaces or tabs inconsistently, or having an incorrect indentation level) is a common syntax error.
- **Using Keywords Incorrectly:** Trying to use a keyword like if as a variable name.

When They Happen:

Syntax errors are typically detected very early:

- **Before Execution (Interpreted Languages):** In languages like Python or JavaScript, the interpreter reads your code before running it. If it finds a syntax error on a specific line, it will often stop and report the error immediately, before executing any code.
- **During Compilation (Compiled Languages):** In languages like Java or C++, the compiler checks all your code for syntax errors *before* creating the executable program. The program won't even compile if there are syntax errors.
- **While Typing (Code Editors):** Many modern code editors (like VS Code) have built-in "linters" or syntax checkers that can highlight syntax errors with underlines or red markers *as you are typing*, which is incredibly helpful!

My early programming days were full of syntax errors. Forgetting a colon in Python, missing a semicolon in JavaScript, or mixing tabs and spaces in Python indentation were common culprits. It felt frustrating initially, but I quickly learned that syntax errors are actually the *easiest* kind of error to fix because the computer usually tells you exactly *where* the problem is and *what* the problem type is.

Identifying and Fixing Syntax Errors:

The key to fixing syntax errors is learning to read the error message provided by the interpreter. Let's look at some examples in Python.

Create a file named syntax_error_example.py with intentional errors:

```
# syntax_error_example.py


# Example 1: Missing colon
```

```
# if 10 > 5
#    print("Ten is greater.")


# Example 2: Typo in keyword
# prnt("Hello again!")


# Example 3: Mismatched quotes
# message = "This string is missing a closing quote



# Example 4: Incorrect indentation
# def my_function():
# print("This line is not indented correctly") # Should be indented


print("Program finished.") # This line might not be reached if an error above
stops execution
```

Save the file. Now, uncomment *one* error example at a time (put # in front of the others) and run the script (python syntax_error_example.py). Observe the error message, then fix it before uncommenting the next error.

Example 1 (Missing Colon):

Uncomment:

```
if 10 > 5
    print("Ten is greater.")
```

Run: python syntax_error_example.py
Output might look like:

```
File "syntax_error_example.py", line 4
    if 10 > 5
             ^
SyntaxError: invalid syntax
```

Reading the Clues:

- File "...", line 4: The error is in this file, on line 4.

- The arrow ^ points to the location *right before* where the interpreter got confused. It saw if $10 > 5$ and was expecting something else right after the 5 (like a colon :) but found the end of the line instead, leading to "invalid syntax".
- SyntaxError: invalid syntax: Tells you the error type and a general message.

Fix: Add the missing colon:

```
if 10 > 5: # Added colon
    print("Ten is greater.")
```

Example 2 (Typo):

Uncomment:

```
prnt("Hello again!")
```

Run: python syntax_error_example.py
Output might look like:

```
File "syntax_error_example.py", line 11
    prnt("Hello again!")
NameError: name 'prnt' is not defined. Did you mean: 'print'?
```

Reading the Clues:

- File "...", line 11: Error on line 11.
- NameError: name 'prnt' is not defined: The interpreter encountered the word prnt and doesn't recognize it as a valid keyword, function name, or variable name in this context.
- Did you mean: 'print'?: Python is often helpful and suggests a possible correction!

Fix: Correct the typo:

```
print("Hello again!") # Corrected typo
```

Example 3 (Mismatched Quotes):

Uncomment:

```
message = "This string is missing a closing quote
```

Run: python syntax_error_example.py
Output might look like:

```
File "syntax_error_example.py", line 18
    message = "This string is missing a closing quote
                  ^
SyntaxError: unterminated string literal (detected at line 18)
```

Reading the Clues:

- File "...", line 18: Error on line 18.
- SyntaxError: unterminated string literal: The error type is SyntaxError. The message says "unterminated string literal", meaning a string was started (with " or ') but never closed.
- (detected at line 18): Confirms the line. The arrow ^ might point to the start of the string.

Fix: Add the missing closing quote:

```
message = "This string is missing a closing quote" # Added closing quote
```

Example 4 (Incorrect Indentation):

Uncomment:

```
def my_function():
print("This line is not indented correctly")
```

Run: python syntax_error_example.py
Output might look like:

```
File "syntax_error_example.py", line 25
    print("This line is not indented correctly")
          ^
IndentationError: expected an indented block after function definition on
line 24
```

Reading the Clues:

- File "...", line 25: The error is on line 25, the print line.
- IndentationError: expected an indented block after function definition on line 24: This error is specific to Python. It clearly states that after the function definition line (line 24), it was expecting the next line (print) to be indented, but it wasn't. The arrow points to the start of the line where the indentation is wrong.

Fix: Indent the line correctly:

```
def my_function():
    print("This line is not indented correctly") # Indented with 4 spaces
(common convention)
```

Commentary: Be careful about mixing spaces and tabs for indentation in Python; configure your code editor to use spaces consistently (typically 4 spaces per level).

My personal strategy for fixing syntax errors is always: 1) **Read the error message.** 2) **Go to the line number.** 3) **Look at the line** *and the line just before it*, paying extra attention to punctuation, quotes, parentheses, and indentation around where the error is reported. 4) **Compare it to correct syntax** for that type of statement (e.g., how should an if statement always look? How should a function definition always look?). Your code editor highlighting errors as you type is also a massive help here!

Syntax errors are frustrating when you're starting because they stop your program dead in its tracks. But they are also the simplest because the computer is directly telling you, "Hey, I don't understand this instruction right here!" The message usually gives you enough information to pinpoint and correct the grammatical mistake.

You've taken a crucial step in becoming a debugger by understanding **Syntax Errors**. You know what they are (grammar mistakes in your code), why they happen (typos, missing punctuation, etc.), and when they are typically detected (before or at the start of execution). Most importantly, you've learned the basic process of **reading error messages and tracebacks** to find the file, line number, and type of syntax error, and how to approach fixing them by looking at the problematic line and its surroundings.

Syntax errors are your first hurdle, and learning to quickly read and fix them is a fundamental skill that builds confidence. Next, we'll look at **Runtime Errors**, which happen *while* your code is running.

11.1.2 Runtime Errors

Alright, you've fixed all your syntax errors. Your code follows the language's rules, and the computer can read your instructions without getting confused about the grammar. Great! But just because an instruction is grammatically correct doesn't mean it's always *possible* to perform that instruction at any given moment during the program's execution.

This is where **Runtime Errors** occur. They happen *while your program is executing*, when the code tries to do something that the computer cannot physically or logically perform with the current data or circumstances. The instruction is understood, but it's currently impossible to complete.

Think back to our recipe analogy. A syntax error was the poorly written instruction itself ("Go kitchen the to"). A runtime error is a grammatically correct instruction that fails in the moment: "Pour the milk into the glass." If, when you try to do this step, you discover there is no milk in the fridge, you will encounter a problem *at the time you try to perform the pouring step*. The instruction itself wasn't wrong, but the *state* of the world (no milk) made it impossible to execute successfully right then.

Why They Happen:

Runtime errors often happen because of:

- **Invalid Data:** Trying to perform an operation on data that's not in the expected format or range (e.g., dividing by zero, converting text that isn't a valid number to an integer).
- **Unavailable Resources:** Trying to open a file that doesn't exist, trying to connect to a network that's down, trying to access a part of memory that's not available.
- **Incorrect State:** Trying to perform an action that's only valid in a specific state (e.g., trying to remove the last item from an empty list).
- **External Issues:** Problems outside your program's direct control (e.g., the database server is down, the internet connection drops).

When They Happen:

Runtime errors happen only *during program execution*, and specifically at the exact line of code where the impossible operation is attempted. The program runs sequentially until it hits that problematic instruction.

My experience with runtime errors often involved not anticipating all the possible things a user might input (like typing letters when I expected numbers), or assuming a file would always exist. It was also a key point where I learned the difference between *valid syntax* and *valid logic at runtime*. The code looked fine, but the data flowing through it caused a crash.

Identifying and Fixing Runtime Errors:

Like syntax errors, runtime errors usually cause the program to stop and produce an error message or traceback. However, the message will indicate a different *type* of error.

Let's revisit our ValueError example from Chapter 9, and also create a ZeroDivisionError and IndexError. Create a file named runtime_error_example.py.

```
# runtime_error_example.py


print("Starting program...")


# Example 1: ValueError (Input conversion failure)
# user_input = input("Enter a whole number: ")
```

```
# number = int(user_input) # This line fails if user enters non-integer text
# print("You entered:", number)

# Example 2: ZeroDivisionError (Division by zero)
# numerator = 10
# denominator = 0
# result = numerator / denominator # This line fails
# print("Result:", result)

# Example 3: IndexError (Accessing outside list range)
# my_list = [1, 2, 3]
# print(my_list[5]) # This line fails because index 5 doesn't exist (valid
indices are 0, 1, 2)

print("Program finished.") # This line might not be reached if an error above
stops execution
```

Save the file. Uncomment *one* error example at a time, and run the script.

Example 1 (ValueError):

Uncomment Example 1. Run: python runtime_error_example.py. When prompted, type hello and press Enter.
Output:

```
Starting program...
Enter a whole number: hello
Traceback (most recent call last):
  File "/path/to/your/project/runtime_error_example.py", line 7, in <module>
    number = int(user_input)
ValueError: invalid literal for int() with base 10: 'hello'
```

Reading the Clues:

- File "...", line 7, in <module>: Tells you where it happened (file and line 7).
- number = int(user_input): Shows the line of code that was executing.
- ValueError: invalid literal for int() with base 10: 'hello': The error type is ValueError. The message explains *why* – the int() function got 'hello' which is an "invalid literal" (invalid text representation) for converting to an integer in base 10.

Fix: This is a data validation problem. You need to ensure the input can be converted *before* attempting the conversion, or handle the potential ValueError. We used try-except in Chapter 9 for this:

```python
user_input = input("Enter a whole number: ")
try:
    number = int(user_input)
    print("You entered:", number)
except ValueError:
    print("That wasn't a valid whole number!") # Handle the error gracefully
```

Example 2 (ZeroDivisionError):

Uncomment Example 2. Run: python runtime_error_example.py.
Output:

```
Starting program...
Traceback (most recent call last):
  File "/path/to/your/project/runtime_error_example.py", line 14, in <module>
    result = numerator / denominator
ZeroDivisionError: division by zero
```

Reading the Clues:

- File "...", line 14, in <module>: Where it happened (line 14).
- result = numerator / denominator: The line of code executing.
- ZeroDivisionError: division by zero: The error type is ZeroDivisionError. The message is clear – you tried to divide by zero, which is mathematically impossible.

Fix: You need to check if the denominator is zero *before* performing the division, using a conditional statement (if):

```python
numerator = 10
denominator = 0
if denominator != 0: # Check if denominator is not zero
    result = numerator / denominator
    print("Result:", result)
else:
    print("Cannot perform division by zero.") # Handle the situation
```

Example 3 (IndexError):

Uncomment Example 3. Run: python runtime_error_example.py.
Output:

```
Starting program...
Traceback (most recent call last):
  File "/path/to/your/project/runtime_error_example.py", line 21, in <module>
    print(my_list[5])
IndexError: list index out of range
```

Reading the Clues:

- File "...", line 21, in <module>: Where it happened (line 21).
- print(my_list[5]): The line of code executing (trying to access index 5).
- IndexError: list index out of range: The error type is IndexError. The message explains why – you tried to access an index (5) that is outside the valid range of indices for this list (0, 1, 2).

Fix: You need to ensure the index you are trying to access is valid for the list's current size, using the len() function and conditional statements, or use a loop that correctly iterates within the valid range.

```
my_list = [1, 2, 3]
index_to_access = 5
if index_to_access < len(my_list): # Check if the index is valid
    print(my_list[index_to_access])
else:
    print(f"Error: Index {index_to_access} is out of range for the list.") #
Handle the error
```

Like Syntax Errors, Runtime Errors provide a traceback that points you to the line of code where the error occurred. The key difference is *what* the error type and message tell you about the *reason* for the error. For runtime errors, it's usually about an invalid *operation* given the current data or circumstances, rather than just a typo in the code's grammar.

My approach to runtime errors is: 1) Read the *type* and *message* of the error at the bottom of the traceback. This tells me the *category* of the problem (invalid value, division by zero, wrong index, etc.). 2) Go to the line number indicated. 3) Look at the variables and operations on that line. 4) Use print() statements *before* that line to see the actual values and data types of the variables involved right before the crash. This usually reveals *why* the operation was impossible (e.g., the variable was 0 when I tried to divide, the list was empty when I tried to access an index, the input string was "hello" when I tried to convert to int).

Runtime errors are more about understanding your data and anticipating possible values or states that could make an operation fail. Using conditional statements (if/else) to check for these problematic conditions *before* attempting the risky operation, or using try-except blocks (Chapter 11) to gracefully handle errors when they occur, are key strategies for writing more robust programs.

You've taken the next step in debugging by understanding **Runtime Errors**. You know what they are (errors occurring during execution due to impossible operations with current data/circumstances), why they happen (invalid data, unavailable resources, incorrect state), and when they occur (at the exact line of the impossible operation). You've seen examples of common runtime errors like ValueError, ZeroDivisionError, and IndexError. You've learned how to use the traceback to find the location and type of the error, and how to use print() statements to inspect variable states *before* the error line to diagnose the cause.

Understanding runtime errors is crucial for writing programs that can handle unexpected data or situations gracefully.

11.1.3 Logic Errors

Alright, you've gotten past the crashes! Your program starts, it runs, it finishes, and it doesn't show you any angry red error messages. Success, right? Well, maybe.

A **Logic Error** is when your program runs without crashing, but the output or behavior is not what you intended. The code is syntactically correct (the grammar is fine), and every operation it attempts is possible at runtime, but the sequence of steps you wrote (your logic) is flawed, leading to an incorrect outcome.

Think back to our cake recipe. A syntax error was the badly written instruction ("Go kitchen the to"). A runtime error was trying to perform a step that was currently impossible ("Pour the milk" when there's no milk). A **logic error** is a recipe that's perfectly readable and performable, but the steps are wrong, resulting in a bad cake ("Add 1 cup of salt instead of 1 cup of sugar"). The person followed the instructions exactly, but the end result is wrong because the instructions themselves contained a mistake in the *logic* of making a cake.

Why They Happen:

Logic errors happen because your understanding of the problem, your plan for solving it, or your translation of that plan into code is incorrect:

- **Flawed Algorithm:** The sequence of steps you designed doesn't actually solve the problem.

- **Incorrect Conditions:** Your if or elif conditions are wrong (e.g., checking age > 18 when you meant age >= 18).
- **Incorrect Loop Logic:** Your loop doesn't run the correct number of times, starts or ends at the wrong point, or processes items in the wrong order.
- **Mistakes in Calculations:** You use the wrong operator or perform operations in the wrong order.
- **Off-by-One Errors:** Loops or list access use an index or count that is one too high or too low.
- **Incorrect Variable Usage:** You use the wrong variable or modify a variable incorrectly within a function or loop.
- **Assuming Data:** You assume input will always be in a certain range or format, and the program misbehaves if it's not (even if it doesn't crash).

When They Happen:

Logic errors don't cause crashes. The program simply runs to completion and gives you a result that is wrong. This makes them harder to find because the computer doesn't give you a helpful error message or line number where the "mistake" occurred – it just shows you the incorrect outcome.

My personal experience with logic errors often involved staring at the correct output (or lack thereof) and thinking, "But *why*?" The program didn't tell me it was wrong; *I* had to figure that out by comparing its output to what I expected. Off-by-one errors in loops or list indexing were particularly frustrating logic errors for me initially.

Identifying and Fixing Logic Errors:

Since there are no error messages for logic errors, finding them relies on careful **testing** and systematic **debugging**.

1. **Testing is Key:** You identify logic errors by **testing your program with different inputs** and comparing the program's output to the output you *expect* based on your understanding of the problem. If the actual output doesn't match the expected output, you have a logic error. This is why the manual verification strategies we discussed in Section 10.5 are so important.
2. **Work Backwards:** Once you know you have a logic error (because the output is wrong for a specific input), you need to work backward from the incorrect output to find the flawed logic in your code.
3. **Use Debugging Techniques Systematically:**
   - **Print Statements:** Sprinkle print() statements throughout your code to track the values of variables and the path of execution. Print values *before* and *after* calculations, *inside* loops, *before* conditional checks, and at

the start and end of functions. See if the values are what you expect them to be at each step. This is often the most effective way to diagnose logic errors.

- o **Simplify Input:** If the program fails for a complex input, try the simplest possible input that still produces the wrong result.
- o **Step Through Code (with a Debugger):** If you're using a debugger (Chapter 11), set breakpoints and step through the code line by line, observing the exact value of every variable at each step. This is very powerful for tracking complex logic.
- o **Isolate the Problem:** If you suspect a specific function or loop, try calling that part of the code with hardcoded test data to see if it produces the correct output in isolation.
- o **Explain Your Code:** Explain your code's logic line by line to yourself, a friend, or even an inanimate object (rubber duck debugging!). This forces you to articulate your assumptions and steps, often revealing the flaw.
- o **Reread the Requirements:** Go back to your initial understanding of the problem or the requirements. Did you misunderstand something? Did you forget to handle a specific case?
- o **Check Conditions and Loops:** Double-check the logic in your if/elif conditions. Are the comparison operators correct? Is the boolean logic (and/or/not) correct? Is your loop starting, ending, and incrementing/decrementing correctly? Are you handling boundary conditions (first item, last item, empty list, zero)?

Let's look at a simple logic error example:

```python
# logic_error_example.py

print("--- Logic Error Example ---")

# Program goal: Calculate the average of a list of numbers

numbers = [10, 20, 30, 40, 50]
total = 0

for number in numbers:
    total = number # LOGIC ERROR: Should be total = total + number or total
+= number

# After the loop, calculate the average
average = total / len(numbers) # This line might not cause a crash

print(f"The list is: {numbers}")
print(f"The calculated total is: {total}")
```

```
print(f"The calculated average is: {average}")
```

Save and run the script.

```
--- Logic Error Example ---
The list is: [10, 20, 30, 40, 50]
The calculated total is: 50
The calculated average is: 10.0
```

Step Explanation: The program ran without crashing. But the output is wrong. The total should be 150, and the average 30.

Debugging Process:

1. *Identify:* The output is wrong. Logic error confirmed.
2. *Hypothesize:* The total or average calculation must be wrong.
3. *Investigate:* Look at the code for the total calculation: total = number. Ah! This line *replaces* the value of total with the current number in each loop iteration. It doesn't *add* the current number to the total. The last number in the loop was 50, so total ended up being 50.
4. *Fix:* Change the line to accumulate the sum.
5. *Test:* Rerun the script with the fix.

```python
# logic_error_example_fixed.py


print("--- Logic Error Example (Fixed) ---")


numbers = [10, 20, 30, 40, 50]
total = 0


for number in numbers:
    total += number # FIX: Use compound assignment to add to the total


average = total / len(numbers)


print(f"The list is: {numbers}")
print(f"The calculated total is: {total}")
print(f"The calculated average is: {average}")
```

Run the fixed script.

```
--- Logic Error Example (Fixed) ---
The list is: [10, 20, 30, 40, 50]
The calculated total is: 150
The calculated average is: 30.0
```

Commentary: The fix involved changing one operator, but identifying the problem required understanding the *intent* (accumulating a sum) and seeing where the code failed to match that intent.

Logic errors are the hardest to find because the computer can't help you locate them directly. They require you to think critically about your own code's logic and use systematic debugging techniques like strategic printing or stepping through code to track the flow and variable values. Testing your code thoroughly with different inputs is your primary way to uncover them.

My personal strategy for logic errors is often to isolate the part I suspect is wrong (a loop, a calculation, a conditional check) and use print() statements to trace the variable values *step-by-step* through that section. For a loop, I'll print the relevant variables at the beginning and end of each iteration. For a conditional, I'll print the variables *before* the if and print messages *inside* each if/elif/else block to see which path is being taken and with what values. This makes the program's hidden execution visible.

You've reached the final frontier of debugging basics: **Logic Errors**. You understand what they are (flawed logic leading to incorrect results without crashing), why they happen (incorrect algorithms, conditions, calculations, etc.), and when they occur (the program runs to completion, but output is wrong). You know that finding them relies on **testing** and using systematic **debugging techniques** like strategic **print statements** to trace code execution and variable values.

Logic errors are challenging, but developing a systematic approach to testing and debugging them is a fundamental skill that distinguishes a beginner from a developer who can build reliable software. You now have the basic tools and understanding to start tackling all three types of errors.

This concludes our look at dealing with mistakes. You've covered all the core fundamental concepts and learned how to troubleshoot. In the final chapter, we'll summarize everything and look ahead to your future in programming.

11.2 Reading and Understanding Error Messages

When your program encounters a Syntax Error or a Runtime Error, the Python interpreter (or the browser's JavaScript console, or a compiler's output) will usually print an **error message** or a **traceback**. This message contains vital clues! Learning to read it is essential.

Let's deliberately create a `ValueError` like we saw in Chapter 9 and look at the message. Create a simple file, `error_example.py`:

```
# error_example.py

print("Starting program...")

age_str = input("Enter your age: ") # User will enter non-number input

# This line will cause a ValueError if age_str is not a valid integer string
age_int = int(age_str)

print("Program finished.")
```

Save the file. Open your terminal, navigate to the directory, and run `python error_example.py`. When prompted, type `hello` and press Enter.

You'll see output similar to this (the exact line numbers and path might differ):

```
Starting program...
Enter your age: hello
Traceback (most recent call last):
  File "/path/to/your/project/error_example.py", line 7, in <module>
    age_int = int(age_str)
ValueError: invalid literal for int() with base 10: 'hello'
```

Let's break down the traceback (the lines starting with `Traceback`):

- **`Traceback (most recent call last):`**: This indicates the start of the traceback, showing the sequence of calls that led to the error. For simple scripts like this, it's usually just one entry.
- **`File "/path/to/your/project/error_example.py", line 7, in <module>`**: This is the most important line for locating the error.
  - o `File "..."`: Tells you the name and location of the file where the error occurred (`error_example.py`).
  - o `line 7`: Tells you the specific line number in that file where the error was detected. Look at line 7 in `error_example.py`.
  - o `in <module>`: Indicates that the error happened in the main part of your script (not inside a function call, which would list the function name here).
- **`age_int = int(age_str)`**: This line shows you the specific code that was being executed when the error occurred.

- **`ValueError: invalid literal for int() with base 10: 'hello'`**: This is the error type and a descriptive message.
  - `ValueError`: Tells you the *type* of error. You can look up `ValueError` in Python documentation if the message isn't clear.
  - `invalid literal for int() with base 10: 'hello'`: This is the error message itself. It tells you *what* went wrong – the `int()` function received a value (`'hello'`) that it couldn't convert into an integer using base 10 numbers.

Reading a traceback means starting from the **bottom** (the error type and message) to understand *what* went wrong, and then looking just above it to see *where* (file and line number) it happened. If you have function calls, the traceback will list each call leading to the error, showing the path of execution (most recent call last).

11.3 Basic Debugging Techniques

Debugging is the process of investigating errors to figure out the root cause and fix it. It's a skill that takes practice, but here are some fundamental techniques:

11.3.1 Using Print Statements / Console Logging

This is the simplest and often most effective technique for beginners (and still widely used by pros!). If you suspect a problem in a certain section of code, add `print()` statements to display the values of variables or confirm that a specific line of code is being reached.

```python
# Debugging with print statements

print("Starting calculation...")

num1_str = input("Enter number 1: ")
num2_str = input("Enter number 2: ")

print(f"DEBUG: num1_str is '{num1_str}', type is {type(num1_str)}") # Print
the input string and its type
print(f"DEBUG: num2_str is '{num2_str}', type is {type(num2_str)}") # Print
the input string and its type


try:
    num1 = int(num1_str)
    num2 = int(num2_str)
```

```
        print(f"DEBUG: Converted num1 to int: {num1}, type is {type(num1)}") #
Print converted value and type
        print(f"DEBUG: Converted num2 to int: {num2}, type is {type(num2)}")

        result = num1 / num2 # Potential for division by zero

        print(f"DEBUG: Calculation performed: {num1} / {num2}") # Confirm
calculation line was reached
        print(f"DEBUG: Result is {result}") # Print the final result

        print("Result:", result)

except ValueError:
        print(f"DEBUG: ValueError occurred. Input was not a valid integer.") #
Confirm which except block was reached
        print("Invalid integer input.")
except ZeroDivisionError: # Python's specific error for division by zero
        print(f"DEBUG: ZeroDivisionError occurred. Tried to divide by {num2}.")
        print("Error: Cannot divide by zero.")

print("Program finished.")
```

Step Explanation: We've added `print()` statements prefixed with "DEBUG" at various points.

- Before conversion: Check the raw input string and its type.
- After conversion: Check the converted number and its type.
- Before and after calculation: Confirm the calculation is attempted and see its result.
- Inside `except` blocks: Confirm which error handler was triggered.

Save and run this script, trying different inputs (valid numbers, text, zero for the second number). Watch the DEBUG messages in the console. They tell you what your program is doing step-by-step and what values variables hold at those points, helping you pinpoint where the error occurs or where the logic goes wrong.

This is my go-to technique for quick debugging. It's simple, works everywhere, and immediately gives you visibility into your program's execution flow and variable states.

11.3.2 Stepping Through Code

Alright, print() statements are your trusty flashlight in the dark alleys of debugging. They let you illuminate specific variable values and check if you're reaching certain parts of your code. But sometimes, especially with complex loops or function calls, you need more control. You need to pause your program exactly when and where you want, look around at *all* your variables, and execute your code one instruction at a time to see the program's state change dynamically.

This is what **stepping through code** with a **debugger** allows you to do.

A debugger is a special tool (often integrated into your code editor or development environment) that lets you control the execution of your program. It's like having a remote control for your running code, with a pause button, a rewind button (sometimes!), and the ability to peek inside the computer's memory.

My personal experience with debuggers was initially intimidating. It felt like a complex tool I didn't need when print() worked okay. But once I learned how to set a breakpoint and step through a loop or a function call, my debugging process became much faster and more effective for tricky issues. It's like upgrading from a flashlight to a high-powered microscope and a pause button for time.

What Stepping Through Code Means:

When you "step through" code with a debugger, you are typically doing the following:

1. **Setting a Breakpoint:** You mark a specific line in your code where you want the program to pause its execution.
2. **Running in Debug Mode:** You start your program using the debugger.
3. **Hitting the Breakpoint:** When the program reaches the line with the breakpoint, it pauses. The terminal output will stop, and your code editor will usually highlight the paused line.
4. **Inspecting Variables:** While paused, the debugger lets you see the current value of *all* variables that are accessible in the current scope. You can hover over variable names, look in a dedicated "Variables" panel, or sometimes type variable names into a "Watch" window or the debugger console.
5. **Stepping Controls:** The debugger provides controls to continue execution:
   - **Continue:** Resume normal program execution until the next breakpoint or the program finishes.
   - **Step Over:** Execute the current line of code, then pause on the *next* line in the same block. If the current line calls a function, Step Over executes the *entire function* and pauses after the function call returns.
   - **Step Into:** If the current line calls a function, Step Into jumps *into* the code of that function and pauses on the first line *inside* the function.
   - **Step Out:** If you are currently inside a function, Step Out executes the rest of the current function's code and pauses on the line *after* the function call returned.
6. **Watching Expressions:** You can often tell the debugger to "watch" the value of a specific variable or even a complex expression as you step through the code, seeing how its value changes line by line.

Why Use Stepping Through Code?

- **Full Visibility:** See the value of *any* variable at a specific point, not just the ones you thought to print.
- **Precise Control:** Pause execution exactly where you need to, even inside loops or nested function calls.
- **Understand Flow:** See the exact path your program takes, line by line, which is invaluable for diagnosing logic errors.
- **Inspect Complex Data:** Easily examine the contents of data structures like lists and dictionaries while paused.

How to Use a Debugger (Conceptual/General Steps):

The exact steps to set up and use a debugger depend heavily on:

- **Your Code Editor:** VS Code, PyCharm, Sublime Text, etc., each have their own debugger interfaces.
- **Your Programming Language:** You need a debugger specifically for the language you're using (e.g., a Python debugger, a JavaScript debugger).
- **Your Project Setup:** Sometimes, complex projects require specific debugger configurations.

However, the general workflow is similar:

1. **Install the Debugger (if needed):** Your code editor might have a built-in debugger for common languages, or you might need to install an extension or plugin for your specific language. For Python in VS Code, the Python extension usually includes a debugger.
2. **Set a Breakpoint:** Open the file you want to debug. Find a line of code where you want the program to pause. Click in the margin next to the line number (usually to the left) to set a breakpoint. A red dot often appears.
3. **Start Debugging:** Find the "Run" or "Debug" menu or icon in your code editor. Select an option like "Start Debugging" or "Run and Debug". You might need to select a specific configuration (e.g., "Python: Current File").
4. **Interact with Your Program:** If your program requires input (like our guessing game), it will run until it hits the input() call. Provide the input in the terminal or a separate debugger console window. The program will continue until the breakpoint.
5. **Use Stepping Controls:** Once paused at the breakpoint, use the debugger's controls (often icons like "play", "step over", "step into", "step out") to move through the code line by line.
6. **Inspect Variables:** As you step, watch the "Variables" panel. You should see the values of variables update as the code executes.
7. **Remove/Add Breakpoints:** You can add or remove breakpoints while the program is paused.
8. **Stop Debugging:** When finished, stop the debugger.

Example Scenario Where Debugging Shines:

Imagine a logic error in a loop from Chapter 6:

```python
# loop_bug.py

numbers = [10, 5, 0, 20]
result = 100

# Intent: Divide 100 by each number in the list
# Problem: What happens when number is 0?

for number in numbers:
    # What is the value of 'number' right before the division?
    # What is the value of 'result' after each step?
    result = result / number # This line will cause a ZeroDivisionError when number is 0

print("Final Result:", result)
```

If you run this with python loop_bug.py, you'll get a ZeroDivisionError and the traceback will point to the line result = result / number. But *why* is number zero?

Using a debugger:

1. Set a breakpoint on the line result = result / number.
2. Start debugging.
3. The program will run, enter the for loop, and pause when number is 10.
4. Inspect variables: number is 10, result is 100.
5. Step Over: result becomes 100 / 10 = 10. Program pauses on the next line (the end of the loop block).
6. Step Over: Loop goes to the next iteration. Program pauses when number is 5.
7. Inspect variables: number is 5, result is 10.
8. Step Over: result becomes 10 / 5 = 2. Program pauses on the next line.
9. Step Over: Loop goes to the next iteration. Program pauses when number is 0.
10. Inspect variables: number is 0, result is 2.
11. Step Over: Execution stops, and the debugger highlights the result = result / number line again, but this time with the ZeroDivisionError.

By stepping through, you *saw* number become 0 just before the problematic line, revealing the cause of the error. You could also see how result changed in each iteration.

Debugging is a more advanced skill than using print statements, but it provides unparalleled visibility into your program's execution and is a crucial tool for tackling complex bugs. Don't feel like you need to master it today, but be aware it exists and makes debugging much more efficient once you're comfortable with the basics.

You've been introduced to a powerful debugging technique: **stepping through code** using a **debugger**. You understand the concept of setting **breakpoints** to pause execution, and using **stepping controls** (step over, step into) to move through code line by line while **inspecting variable values**. You saw how this provides more control and visibility than print() statements alone, although print() remains a fundamental debugging tool. You also understand that the exact implementation depends on your environment but the core principles are universal.

This completes our look at debugging basics. You now have tools and strategies to approach finding and fixing all types of errors you'll encounter. In the final chapter, we'll summarize everything you've learned and look ahead to your exciting future in programming.

11.4 Strategies for Fixing Bugs

Finding the bug (debugging) is half the battle; fixing it is the other. Here are some strategies:

- **Stay Calm and Patient:** Frustration is normal, but panic doesn't help. Approach debugging like a puzzle.
- **Read the Error Message Carefully:** Don't just look at the red text and give up. Read the error *type* and the *message*. Google the error message if needed.
- **Go to the Line Number:** The traceback gives you the file and line number. Go there and look at the code. What is happening on that line? What are the variables involved?
- **Form Hypotheses:** Based on the error and the line of code, *guess* what might be wrong. "Maybe `age_str` isn't what I expected it to be?" "Maybe `num2` is zero at this moment?"
- **Test Your Hypotheses:** Use `print()` statements (or a debugger) to verify your guesses. Print the values of variables *just before* the line that failed. Did the variable have the value you expected? Was it the correct data type?
- **Isolate the Problem:** If you have a complex program, try to isolate the part that's failing. Can you comment out other code? Can you call the problematic function with simplified inputs?
- **Explain the Code (to yourself or someone else):** Try explaining line by line what you *think* the code is doing. Often, explaining it out loud helps you spot the flawed logic. Rubber duck debugging (explaining your code to an inanimate object) is a real and surprisingly effective technique!

- **Check Your Assumptions:** Are you assuming the user will always enter a valid number? Are you assuming a list will never be empty? Logic errors often come from incorrect assumptions.
- **Consult Resources:** Look at the language's documentation for the function or operator causing the error. Search online for the error message; chances are, someone else has encountered it! Ask for help in online communities (providing your code, the error message, and what you've tried).

Debugging is an iterative process. You'll make a guess, test it, learn something new, form a new guess, and repeat until you find the root cause. It's a fundamental skill that you will continuously improve throughout your programming career. Embracing it and developing a systematic approach will make you a much more effective programmer.

You've faced the inevitable: errors! You now understand the difference between **syntax errors**, **runtime errors**, and **logic errors**. You know how to approach **reading error messages** and tracebacks to locate issues. You've learned the invaluable technique of using **print statements** for basic debugging and strategies for **fixing bugs** by approaching them systematically, testing hypotheses, and using resources.

Dealing with mistakes is not a sign of failure; it's part of the process. By learning these debugging basics, you are equipped to find and fix problems in your code, which is essential for building reliable software.

You've now covered all the core fundamental concepts of programming and learned how to troubleshoot common issues. In the final chapter, we'll summarize everything you've learned and look ahead to the exciting next steps in your programming journey!

Chapter 12
The Journey Ahead: What's Next?

Alright, future software developer, you've made it! You've read the chapters, written the code, encountered errors, and hopefully built your first small program. Take a moment to celebrate this milestone! You have officially taken your first steps into programming.

Remember the feeling of looking at code as a mysterious language? You've started to decode it. You've learned the basic grammar (syntax), the vocabulary (keywords, variable names), how to work with different types of information (data types, data structures), how to perform actions (operators, functions), and how to control the flow of instructions (decisions, loops). You've learned how to communicate with the user (input/output) and how to approach problem-solving and fixing mistakes (debugging).

My personal journey into programming started with a single language and a few basic problems, much like this book covers. The excitement came from realizing that these same core concepts were the building blocks for *everything* – websites, mobile apps, games, scientific simulations. It felt like learning a universal language that could be applied to almost any challenge in the digital world. And that's the power you now hold.

12.1 What You Have Learned

Take a moment to celebrate! You've reached the final chapter of this book, and that means you've successfully navigated the essential, fundamental concepts of computer programming. This wasn't just a casual read; you've learned a new way of thinking and gained the basic tools to start building software. That is genuinely impressive!

Think back to when you first opened this book. The idea of writing code might have felt abstract or even a little daunting. You've moved beyond that. You now understand what code *is* – not some mysterious magic, but a set of precise instructions you write for a computer. You've learned how computers execute those instructions, whether through interpretation or compilation, and the importance of following the specific rules (syntax) of a programming language.

You've mastered the fundamental ways programs handle information. You know how to use **variables** as containers to store different kinds of data, and you understand the basic **data types** like numbers, text (strings), and True/False values (booleans). You also got an introduction to organizing collections of this data using basic **data structures** like lists (ordered sequences) and dictionaries (key-value pairs) – a crucial step beyond handling just single pieces of information.

Beyond just storing data, you've learned how to *work* with it. You understand **operators** – the symbols and keywords that let you perform calculations (like adding numbers) and make comparisons (like checking if one value is greater than another), which give you those essential boolean results.

Crucially, you've learned the core concepts of **control flow**, the fundamental way programs alter their execution path. You know how to make your programs **make decisions** using **conditional statements** (`if`, `elif`, `else`), executing different blocks of code based on whether a condition is true or false. And you know how to make your programs **repeat actions** efficiently using **loops** (`for`, `while`), saving you from writing the same code over and over. You even learned how to use `break` and `continue` to control loop execution and the importance of avoiding infinite loops.

You've seen how to organize these instructions into reusable blocks using **functions**. You know how to define a function, give it a name, specify what information it needs to receive (its parameters), write the code it executes, and how to get a result back from it (`return`). This ability to structure your code into functions is vital for building programs that are readable and maintainable.

You've made your programs interactive! You understand the basic cycle of **input and output** – how to show information to the user (using `print()`) and how to get information *from* the user (using `input()`), including the critical skill of understanding that input is often initially a string and needs **type casting** (like converting text to a number) before it can be fully processed.

And you didn't just learn concepts in isolation. You applied them by **building your first piece of software** as a mini-project, seeing how variables, control flow, input/output, and functions work together to create a complete, if simple, program. This practical application is where the theoretical concepts truly come to life.

Finally, you've begun to understand the practical realities of coding – that errors are normal. You've learned about the different types of errors (syntax, runtime, logic), how to start **reading error messages** and tracebacks, and basic **debugging techniques** like using print statements to figure out where and why your code isn't working. This skill in troubleshooting is just as important as writing the code itself.

These concepts – variables, operators, control flow (decisions and loops), functions, data structures, input/output, problem-solving, and debugging – are the universal language of programming. They are the core ideas that form the foundation for writing code in *any* language, for *any* purpose. You've not just learned *some* programming; you've learned the *fundamentals* of programming.

That realization, that the core skills I was building were transferable and applicable far beyond the specific exercises I was doing, was a major turning point in my own learning. It showed me that the effort I was putting in wasn't just for one small script; it was an investment in my ability to build almost anything I could imagine in the digital world.

You've built a strong base. You understand the essential concepts and how they fit together to create functioning software. This puts you in a fantastic position to continue your journey. In the next sections of this final chapter, we'll reflect on the power you now hold and look at the exciting possibilities for where you can take your programming skills next.

12.2 Exploring Different Programming Domains

Alright, you've got the fundamental concepts down. You know variables, loops, decisions, functions – the core logic of programming. That's like knowing basic grammar and vocabulary. Now, where do you apply that knowledge? What kind of "sentences" or "stories" do you want to write with your code?

Programming isn't just one job title or one type of software. It's a vast field with many different areas of specialization, often called **programming domains**. Each domain uses the same fundamental concepts you've learned, but applies them to solve different kinds of problems, uses specific languages and tools, and requires learning domain-specific knowledge.

Think of it this way: knowing English grammar lets you write novels, scientific papers, movie scripts, or advertising copy. Each of those requires the same basic language skills but applies them in a specific context with unique vocabulary and styles. Similarly, your programming fundamentals let you write web applications, mobile apps, data analysis tools, or games.

My personal journey involved starting with simple scripting, then moving into back-end web development. Friends of mine took the same basic programming class but went into mobile app development or data analysis. The core skills are the same, but the paths diverge based on interest and the type of problems you want to solve. It's exciting to see how the same principles manifest in completely different kinds of software!

Let's explore some of the most common programming domains you might consider after learning the fundamentals.

12.2.1 Web Development (Front-end, Back-end)

This is one of the largest and most visible domains. Web developers build the websites and web applications you use every day (like social media, online stores, news sites, streaming services). Web development is often split into two main areas:

- **Front-end Development:** As discussed in the introduction to this book, this is the part of the website that runs in the user's browser. It's everything the user *sees* and *interacts with* directly. The core languages are HTML (structure), CSS (styling), and JavaScript (interactivity). Front-end developers often use modern JavaScript frameworks/libraries like **React**, **Vue.js**, or **Angular** to build complex, dynamic user interfaces efficiently. If you enjoyed the HTML, CSS, and JavaScript chapters of this book and like creating visual, interactive experiences, front-end might be for you.
    - *Example Task:* Building a user interface for an online store, ensuring it looks good on phones and desktops, validating form input before sending it to the server, creating smooth animations.

- o *Common Languages/Tools:* HTML, CSS, JavaScript, TypeScript, React, Vue, Angular, Webpack, npm.
- **Back-end Development:** This is the "behind-the-scenes" part that runs on servers. It handles storing and managing data (databases), processing logic, user authentication, and providing data to the front-end (via APIs). Back-end languages are diverse and include **Python** (using frameworks like Django or Flask), **JavaScript** (using Node.js), **Java** (Spring), **Ruby** (Rails), **Go**, **PHP**, etc. If you're more interested in data management, server logic, and building APIs, back-end might be a good fit.
  - o *Example Task:* Creating a user registration system, building an API to provide product information to the front-end, securely storing user data, handling payment processing.
  - o *Common Languages/Tools:* Python, JavaScript (Node.js), SQL, Django, Flask, Express, Ruby on Rails, databases (PostgreSQL, MySQL, MongoDB).

Commentary: Many developers specialize in either front-end or back-end, but "full-stack" developers work on both. Your programming fundamentals are essential for either path!

12.2.2 Mobile App Development

This domain is about building applications that run on smartphones and tablets (iOS and Android).

- **Native Development:** Building apps specifically for one platform using its native language and tools. This often provides the best performance and access to device features.
  - o *iOS:* Uses **Swift** or Objective-C, with Apple's Xcode development environment.
  - o *Android:* Uses **Kotlin** or Java, with Google's Android Studio environment.
- **Cross-Platform Development:** Using frameworks that allow you to write code once and deploy to both iOS and Android. This can be faster and more cost-effective but might involve some trade-offs compared to native development.
  - o Popular frameworks include **React Native** (uses JavaScript/React) and **Flutter** (uses the Dart language).

Commentary: If you're excited about building apps people use on their phones and tablets, mobile development is a great area. Your understanding of variables, control flow, functions, and data structures is directly applicable.

12.2.3 Data Science and Machine Learning

This domain involves analyzing large datasets, extracting insights, building statistical models, and creating systems that can learn from data (Machine Learning).

- Data scientists use programming to clean, transform, analyze, and visualize data. Machine Learning engineers build and deploy models.

- This field relies heavily on mathematical and statistical concepts.
- It often uses specialized libraries built on top of general-purpose languages.
- *Example Task:* Analyzing sales data to identify trends, building a model to predict customer behavior, processing large datasets for research.
- *Common Languages/Tools:* **Python** (with libraries like Pandas, NumPy, Matplotlib, seaborn, scikit-learn, TensorFlow, PyTorch), **R**, SQL.

Commentary: If you enjoy working with numbers, statistics, finding patterns, and solving problems using data, this domain could be a great fit. Python's versatility makes it a popular choice here.

12.2.4 Game Development

Building video games! This domain can range from simple 2D games to complex 3D simulations.

- Often involves using game engines (like Unity or Unreal Engine) which provide tools for graphics, physics, and interaction.
- Requires understanding game loops (a type of continuous repetition!), physics, graphics, and user input in a real-time environment.
- *Example Task:* Programming player movement, implementing game rules, creating enemy AI, handling scoring.
- *Common Languages/Tools:* **C++** (especially for performance/engines), **C#** (Unity engine), **Python** (scripting, simple games), scripting languages specific to engines.

Commentary: If you're passionate about games and enjoy the blend of logic, creativity, and often visual programming, exploring game development can be very rewarding.

12.2.5 Automation and Scripting

This domain is about writing small programs (scripts) to automate repetitive tasks on a computer or server, process files, manage systems, or connect different software tools.

- Scripts are often shorter and less complex than full applications but save significant time on manual tasks.
- Used heavily in system administration, IT, and for personal productivity.
- *Example Task:* Automatically renaming hundreds of files, downloading data from a website periodically, sending automated reports, setting up software on a server.
- *Common Languages/Tools:* **Python**, Bash (Linux/macOS command line scripting), PowerShell (Windows command line scripting), Ruby.

Commentary: If you find yourself doing the same task repeatedly on your computer, scripting is a practical way to immediately see the benefit of coding by automating that task. Python is very popular for general-purpose scripting.

12.2.6 Other Domains (Briefly)

Many other domains exist, including:

- **Embedded Systems & Robotics:** Programming microcontrollers and hardware (C, C++, Rust, Python).
- **Cybersecurity:** Writing tools for security analysis, penetration testing, or defense (Python, C, C++).
- **Cloud Computing:** Working with cloud platforms like AWS, Google Cloud, Azure (involves scripting, infrastructure-as-code tools).
- **Database Administration:** Managing databases (SQL).

This list isn't exhaustive, but it gives you a taste of the variety of ways programming skills are applied.

My advice when looking at these domains is to explore! Read articles, watch introductory videos, and try small tutorials in areas that pique your interest. The fundamentals you've learned are valuable everywhere.

You've now got a panoramic view of the programming landscape! You understand that your foundational skills are applicable across diverse domains like web development (front-end and back-end), mobile apps, data science, game development, and automation. You know some of the key languages and technologies associated with each.

This exploration helps you think about what kind of problems you want to solve with code and what direction you might want to take your learning next. Remember, the fundamental concepts you learned in this book are your passport to explore any of these exciting fields. Now that we've looked ahead, we'll wrap things up in the final chapter, summarizing your journey and providing resources for your continued growth.

12.3 Choosing Your Next Language or Framework

After mastering the fundamentals, you might want to pick a specific language or framework and go deeper. How do you choose?

- **Based on Your Interests:** What kind of software excites you most? If you love building interactive visuals, explore front-end web development (JavaScript + HTML/CSS). If you're fascinated by data, look into data science (Python + libraries). If you want to build mobile apps, explore mobile development languages or frameworks.
- **Based on Career Goals:** Research programming jobs in your area or the fields you're interested in. Which languages and frameworks are most in demand?

- **Based on Community and Resources:** Choose a language or framework with a large, active community and lots of tutorials, documentation, and courses available for beginners. Python and JavaScript are excellent here.
- **Just Pick One:** Don't fall into "tutorial hell" by jumping between languages without going deep. Pick one path that seems interesting and stick with it for a while to build proficiency. Remember, once you know the fundamentals, learning another language is mostly about learning new syntax and libraries, not completely new concepts.

If you used Python for the examples in this book, continuing with Python (exploring libraries like Django or Flask for web, or Pandas for data) is a natural next step. If web interactivity in the browser sparked your interest, diving into JavaScript, the DOM more deeply, and then a framework like React or Vue is a great path.

12.4 The Importance of Community

Programming doesn't have to be a solitary activity. The programming community is vast, supportive, and filled with resources.

- **Online Forums:** Websites like Stack Overflow are invaluable for getting answers to coding questions (learn how to ask good questions!).
- **Online Communities:** Discord servers, Reddit communities (like r/learnprogramming, r/Python, r/javascript), and online forums dedicated to specific languages or technologies are great places to connect with other learners and experienced developers.
- **Meetups:** Check for local programming meetups in your area. Connecting with people in person can be very motivating.
- **Contributing to Open Source:** Once you're more comfortable, contributing to open-source projects is a great way to learn from experienced developers and build your skills.

Don't hesitate to seek help when you're stuck or share your own progress. Being part of a community makes the learning process more enjoyable and sustainable.

12.5 Continuing Your Learning Journey

Becoming a proficient programmer is a continuous journey. Technology evolves, and there's always something new to learn.

- **Build Projects:** Keep building things! Start small, and gradually take on more complex projects. This is the best way to learn and build a portfolio.
- **Read Code:** Read code written by others (open source projects are great for this). See how experienced developers solve problems and structure their code.

- **Never Stop Asking "Why":** Don't just memorize syntax. Understand the concepts behind why things work. Why use a loop here? Why is this data structure appropriate? Why choose this function over another?
- **Learn Data Structures and Algorithms:** While this book introduced basic structures, computer science has a richer vocabulary of data structures and algorithms that are crucial for building efficient and scalable software.
- **Understand Computer Science Fundamentals:** Concepts like how computers work at a deeper level, memory management, and computational complexity are valuable as you progress.

This book has given you the essential keys to unlock the door to programming. The path ahead is filled with exciting challenges and endless opportunities to build and create.

Conclusion

Alright, you've made it to the finish line of "Your First Steps into Programming"! Take a moment and let that sink in. You've gone from potentially knowing nothing about coding to understanding the fundamental concepts that power almost all software. That is a significant achievement, a testament to your curiosity and persistence.

When I look back at my own beginning, I remember feeling overwhelmed by the sheer volume of things there seemed to be to learn. But focusing on the core principles, the "why" behind the syntax, made the journey feel less like memorizing a dictionary and more like learning how to think in a new way. And that's what I hope this book has helped you do.

You are no longer just a user of software; you have taken your first steps towards becoming a creator of it.

Summary of Fundamentals Learned

Let's quickly recap the essential building blocks you've learned throughout this book. Think of these as the core tools in your new programmer's toolbox:

- **What Programming Is:** You now understand that coding is about writing precise, step-by-step instructions for a computer to execute, and that the programmer's role is primarily that of a problem-solver and translator.
- **Your Development Environment:** You know how to set up a basic workspace, choose a code editor, navigate the command line (or terminal), and the fundamental process of writing, saving, and running a script.
- **Variables and Data Types:** You understand how to store different kinds of information (numbers, text/strings, booleans) in variables and how to choose meaningful names for them.
- **Operators:** You know how to perform actions on your data – arithmetic calculations, assigning values, comparing values (==, >, etc.) to get boolean results, and combining boolean results using logical operators (and, or, not).
- **Control Flow (Decisions):** You learned how to make your program choose different paths based on conditions using if, elif, and else statements.
- **Control Flow (Repetition):** You learned how to make your program repeat actions efficiently using for and while loops.
- **Functions:** You understand how to organize reusable blocks of code into functions, giving them inputs (parameters) and getting outputs (return values), which makes your programs more modular and readable.
- **Data Structures:** You learned how to organize collections of data using fundamental structures like Lists (ordered sequences) and Dictionaries (key-value pairs).

- **Input and Output:** You know how to make your programs interactive by showing information to the user (`print`) and getting information *from* the user (`input`), including the crucial step of handling input data types (type casting) and basic error awareness.
- **Building Software:** You've applied these concepts together in a mini-project, seeing how all the pieces collaborate in a complete program.
- **Handling Mistakes:** You've faced errors, learned about different types of bugs, how to start reading error messages, and basic debugging techniques like using print statements.

These concepts are the core of programming logic. They are not tied to any single language, operating system, or type of software. They are the universal truths of telling a computer what to do.

Your Power to Build Software

Before picking up this book, the idea of building software might have felt like something only experienced developers could do. Now, you've actually done it! You've written instructions, solved a small problem, and created a working program.

That experience, even for a simple guessing game, is invaluable. It proves to you that you *can* translate your ideas into code. You have taken a concept from your mind and manifested it as functioning software. This power to build, to create, and to automate is what makes programming so exciting and rewarding.

This book hasn't made you an expert (that comes with years of practice!), but it has given you the foundational understanding and the essential tools to continue learning and building. You understand the core ideas, and that makes learning anything else in the programming world significantly easier.

Resources for Continued Growth

Your programming journey is just beginning! To continue building on this foundation, make use of these resources (detailed in the Appendices):

- **The Glossary:** Refer back to this whenever you encounter a term you're unsure about.
- **Basic Syntax Reference:** Keep this handy as you write more code; it's easy to forget exact syntax rules when you're starting out.
- **Recommended Resources and Communities:** This is perhaps the most important appendix for your next steps.
    - **Official Documentation:** Learn how to find and use the official documentation for the language(s) you use. It's the most authoritative source of information.
    - **Online Tutorials and Courses:** Many excellent free and paid resources are available to learn specific languages, frameworks, and concepts in more depth.

- **Coding Practice Websites:** Sites like Codecademy, freeCodeCamp, HackerRank, LeetCode (for later) offer interactive coding exercises and challenges to hone your skills.
- **Online Communities:** Connect with other programmers on forums, chat platforms, and social media. Asking questions, sharing your progress, and seeing what others are doing is incredibly helpful.
- **Open Source Projects:** Look at code on platforms like GitHub. Seeing how experienced developers write real-world code is a great learning experience.

My advice for these next steps? **Keep coding!** Find small problems around you that you could solve with a script. Build variations of the mini-project. Don't be afraid to try building something you're not quite sure how to do yet – figuring it out is part of the learning process. And remember, every programmer started exactly where you are. Be patient with yourself, stay curious, and celebrate your progress.

Thank you for letting me guide you through your first steps into programming. It's an incredible skill that can change how you interact with the world and empower you to build your own solutions.

You have the fundamentals. You have the resources. Now, go forth and build software! The digital world is ready for your creations.